FREE TRADE:
The Necessary Foundation
for World Peace

D1606700

FREE TRADE:

The Necessary Foundation for World Peace

edited by Joan Kennedy Taylor

The Foundation for Economic Education, Inc.
Irvington-on-Hudson, New York 10533

"A National Policy for Peace" (p. iii–v) and "The Economics of War" (pp. 77–83) are excerpted from *Human Action,* ©1949 by Ludwig von Mises and are used with permission of Contemporary Books, Inc., Chicago.

Published April 1986

ISBN-0-910614-71-7

TABLE OF CONTENTS

Introduction

The issue here concerns voluntary exchange among individuals in contrast to a governmental policy of protectionism. This problem is as old as civilization and has been much debated. Yet, it persists and flares anew as in our time. So there is need to review what careful scholars have had to say on this matter. The selections in this volume are from previously published articles, many from the pages of *The Freeman*.

Before entering into the specifics of free trade and protectionism, it is appropriate to consider the nature of man and of government. Why do we behave as we do, often trying to satisfy our wants through individual or collectivized force? And what is the proper role of government?

The size and scope of government depends directly or indirectly on the extent to which individuals rely upon coercive force against others to try to satisfy their wants.

The purpose of forcible action is to overpower, and the prevailing power in a society is the effective government at any given time. Coercion as such carries no built-in regulator or means of self-restraint. The tendency of government is to grow.

Noting how government grows in power has led some persons to conclude that governments are the cause of violence among men and that peace would reign if all governmental structures were dismantled. What these persons fail to see is that human nature is the source of violence among us and there is more to changing human nature than simply ridding ourselves of the governmental trappings.

Despite the outstanding efforts of the Founding Fathers of the United States to diffuse and limit government power, we note the modern drift toward socialism. That the limits are being violated and exceeded in our time is neither to discredit the Founders nor is it necessarily a reflection on those now holding political office.

Our big government simply measures the extent to which the people have come to rely on coercion in their relationships. Government grows in proportion to such violence—or faces displacement by a superior power. So, if we want less government intervention, we must rid ourselves of our violent natures.

As we survey the supposedly domestic interventions of the advanced welfare state we see that many of these have international consequences that lead to war. For instance, subsidized ocean and air transport, farm price supports, trade agreements, tariff policies and similar interventions breed foreign antagonism that leads nations to the brink, and then to war.

If violence is in our nature, and not necessarily a consequence of government, then we should try to curb this tendency. Reasonable men will try to abide by just and peaceful rules of conduct and look to government for defense only. Its purpose would be to suppress any outbreak of violence, fraud or coercive threat against the life or property of any peaceful person.

Much as we might applaud the Founding Fathers' ideal of limited government, there is still the temptation to pervert the laws to our own selfish advantage. Hence the ongoing conflict between the policies of free trade and those of protectionism.

One of the earlier manifestations of protectionism came under the name of "mercantilism." This was the problem Adam Smith tackled in *The Wealth of Nations* published in 1776—the problem that flared into war in the American colonies that same year.

For a further explanation of protectionism and its consequences, see the chapter on "The Mercantile Impasse" (page 41). Other examples of the way domestic welfare programs breed international conflict are highlighted in chapters on agricultural subsidies (page 56) and labor union tactics (page 63).

As Adam Smith recognized, and as market economists have since confirmed, the foundations of peaceful foreign policy rest on free trade—reliance domestically and internationally on the competitive market economy. So, in a sense, the publication of *The Wealth of Nations* opened up the rationale for peace instead of conflict. But even when the course is clearly marked, thoughtless persons seek short cuts and special intervention for their protection. So grows the welfare state. And from such measures of political control are reaped the terrible consequences of war. This selection of essays is offered as warning against warlike behavior and argument for the peaceful alternative of trade.

Beyond resort to force for defense, peaceful persons would look to their own efforts, and to voluntary exchange through service to others, to satisfy their own wants. Their hope for a better world or a better society would be through self-improvement rather than the reform of other persons. Self-improvement is a do-it-yourself project without violence toward others; it affords an example others may follow without provoking their violent retaliation. It broadens the path to liberty, diminishes the need for government. It is the key to peace.

PAUL L. POIROT

Prologue

A National Policy for Peace

by Ludwig von Mises

T he conflict between the have-nots and the haves is a real conflict. But it is present only in a world in which any sovereign government is free to hurt the interest of all peoples—its own included—by depriving the consumers of the advantages a better exploitation of this country's resources would give them. It is not sovereignty as such that makes for war, but sovereignty of governments not entirely committed to the principles of the market economy.

Liberalism did not and does not build its hopes upon abolition of the sovereignty of the various national governments, a venture which would result in endless wars. It aims at a general recognition of the idea of economic freedom. If all people become liberal and conceive that economic freedom best serves their own interests, national sovereignty will no longer engender conflict and war. What is needed to make peace durable is neither international treaties and covenants nor international tribunals and organizations like the defunct League of Nations or its successor, the United Nations. If the principle of the market economy is universally accepted, such makeshifts are unnecessary; if it is not accepted, they are futile. Durable peace can only be the outgrowth of a change in ideologies. As long as the peoples cling to the Montaigne dogma and think that they cannot prosper economically except at the expense of other nations, peace will never be anything other than a period of preparation for the next war.

Protectionism Leads to Strife

Economic nationalism is incompatible with durable peace. Yet economic nationalism is unavoidable where there is government interference with business. Protectionism is indispensable where there is no domestic free trade. Where there is government interference with business, free trade even in the short run would frustrate the aims sought by the various interventionist measures.

It is an illusion to believe that a nation would lastingly tolerate other nations' policies which harm the vital interest of its own citizens. Let us assume that the United Nations had been established in the year 1600 and that the Indian tribes of North America had been admitted as members of this organization. Then the sovereignty of these Indians would have been recognized as inviolable. They would have been given the right to exclude all aliens from entering their territory and from exploiting its rich natural resources which they themselves did not know how to utilize. Does anybody really believe that any international covenant or charter could have prevented the Europeans from invading these countries?

Many of the richest deposits of various mineral substances are located in areas whose inhabitants are too ignorant, too inert, or too dull to take advantage of the riches nature has bestowed upon them. If the governments of these countries prevent aliens from exploiting these deposits, or if their conduct of public affairs is so arbitrary that no foreign investments are safe, serious harm is inflicted upon all those foreign peoples whose material well-being could be improved by a more adequate utilization of the deposits concerned. It does not matter whether the policies of these governments are the outcome of a general cultural backwardness or of the adoption of the now fashionable ideas of interventionism and economic nationalism. The result is the same in both cases.

There is no use in conjuring away these conflicts by wishful thinking. What is needed to make peace durable is a change in ideologies. What generates war is the economic philosophy almost universally espoused today by governments and political parties. As this philosophy sees it, there prevail within the unhampered market economy irreconcilable conflicts between the interests of various nations. Free trade harms a nation; it brings about impoverishment. It is the duty of government to prevent the evils of free trade by trade barriers. We may, for the sake of argument, disregard the fact that protectionism also hurts the interests of the nations which resort to it. But there can be no doubt that protectionism aims at damaging the interests of foreign peoples and really does damage them. It is an illusion to assume that those injured will tolerate other nations' protectionism if they believe that they are strong enough to brush it away by the use of arms. The philosophy of protectionism is a philosophy of war. The wars of our age are not at variance with popular economic doctrines; they are, on the contrary, the inescapable result of a consistent application of these doctrines.

The League of Nations did not fail because its organization was deficient. It failed because it lacked the spirit of genuine liberalism. It was a convention of governments imbued with the spirit of economic nationalism and entirely committed to the principles of economic warfare. While the delegates indulged in mere academic talk about good will among the nations, the governments whom they represented inflicted a good deal of evil upon all other nations. The two decades of the League's functioning were marked by each nation's adamant economic warfare against all other nations. The tariff protectionism of the years before 1914 was mild indeed when compared with what developed in the 'twenties and 'thirties—viz., embargoes, quantitative trade control, foreign exchange control, monetary devaluation, and so on.

The prospects for the United Nations are not better, but rather worse. Every nation looks upon imports, especially upon imports of manufactured goods, as upon a disaster. It is the avowed goal of almost all countries to bar foreign manufacturers as much as possible from access to their domestic markets. Almost all nations are fighting against the specter of an unfavorable balance of trade. They do not want to cooperate; they want to protect themselves against the alleged dangers of cooperation.

Part One

What's Wrong With Protectionism

"The philosophy of protectionism is a philosophy of war," said Ludwig von Mises in the excerpt from *Human Action* that stands as a Prologue to this book. It is that philosophy that this book intends to analyze and combat, by bringing together these essays—originally published as long ago as 1847 and as recently as 1985—which have been selected to cast light on the contributions that free trade policies can make toward a durable peace.

Today you will find neoliberals and neoconservatives who support the economics of free trade, as well as classical liberals, libertarians, and conservatives. But this is often a shaky alliance, vulnerable to the pleadings of special circumstance and the perceived threat of war. A free-trade policy is seen by many as a luxury in which we can indulge ourselves when things are going well internationally. This leads politicians to hesitate to divest the United States of the ability to wage economic warfare; which means, to devise schemes to prosper at the expense of other countries, which means, to be protectionist. And until we are willing to abandon economic warfare as a viable alternative, as Mises says in our Prologue, "peace will never be anything other than a period of preparation for the next war."

The essays in Part One introduce us to our subject matter. Frank Chodorov offers an overview of the importance of trade in human life: the ways in which it brings diverse cultures together, and the isolation and suspicion that result from impediments to trade. W. M. Curtiss makes the combined economic and moral argument that places the consumer at the center of the discussion. Bettina Bien Greaves sketches in the political history of protectionism in the U.S. from the Tariff Act of 1789 to President Kennedy's Message to Congress in January of 1962. She goes on to review the arguments that have made protectionism seem spuriously appealing, and the economic analysis underlying the free trade position, especially the arguments against economic nationalism. In the last selection, an essay from Frederic Bastiat's *Economic Sophisms* zeroes in on the primary tenet of economic nationalism—the fallacious argument that the nation that exports industrial products is dominating the nation that imports those products and is making such a nation dependent. Taken together, these four essays are meant to establish a foundation upon which the rest of the book will build.

1

The Humanity of Trade

by Frank Chodorov

Frank Chodorov (1887–1966), who turned his hand to a number of occupations before he discovered the philosophy of freedom by reading the works of Henry George, is perhaps best remembered today as an editor and individualist writer. His books include One is a Crowd *and* The Income Tax: Root of All Evil, *and he was the founder and editor of the journal* analysis *in 1950 and editor of* The Freeman *in 1954–55. In this essay, first published in* The Freeman *in July, 1956, he stresses the point that trade leaves everyone better off, and indeed, unhampered trade is crucial to a full enjoyment of life. He also sounds the central theme of this book: interference with the free flow of trade is analogous to an act of war and, he speculates, "Perhaps the removal of trade restrictions throughout the world would do more for the cause of universal peace than can any political union of peoples separated by trade barriers."*

Wherever two boys swap tops for marbles, that is the market place. The simple barter is in terms of human happiness no different from a trade transaction involving banking operations, insurance, ships, railroads, wholesale and retail establishments; for in any case the effect and purpose of trade is to make up a lack of satisfactions. The boy with a pocketful of marbles is handicapped in the enjoyment of life by his lack of tops, while the other is similarly discomfited by his need for marbles; both have a better time of it after the swap, while their respective surpluses before the swap are nuisances. In like manner, the Detroit worker who has helped to pile up a heap of automobiles in the warehouse is none the better off for his efforts until the product has been shipped to Brazil in exchange for his morning cup of coffee. Trade is nothing but the release of what one has in abundance in order to obtain some other thing he wants. It is as pertinent for the buyer to say "thank you" as for the seller.

The market place is not necessarily a specific site, although every trade must

3

take place somewhere. It is more exactly a system of channeling goods or services from one worker to another, from fabricator to consumer, from where a superfluity exists to where there is a need. It is a method devised by man in his pursuit of happiness to diffuse satisfactions, and operating only by the human instinct of value. Its function is not only to transfer ownership from one person to another, but also to direct the current of human exertion; for the price-indicator on the chart of the market place registers the desires of people, and the intensity of these desires, so that other people (looking to their own profit) may know how best to employ themselves.

Living without trade may be possible, but it would hardly be living; at best it would be mere existence. Until the market place appears, men are reduced to getting by with what they can find in nature in the way of food and raiment; nothing more. But the will to live is not merely a craving for existence; it is rather an urge to reach out in all directions for a fuller enjoyment of life, and it is by trade that this inner drive achieves some measure of fulfillment. The greater the volume and fluidity of market place transactions the higher the wage-level of Society; and, insofar as things and services make for happiness, the higher the wage-level the greater the fund of happiness.

Tangible and Intangible Riches

The importance of the market place to the enjoyment of life is illustrated by a custom recorded by Franz Oppenheimer in *The State*. In ancient times, on days designated as holy, the market place and its approaches were held inviolable even by professional robbers; in fact, stepping out of character, these robbers acted as policemen for the trade routes, seeing to it that merchants and caravans were not molested. Why? Because they had accumulated a superfluity of loot of one kind, more than they could consume, and the easiest way of transmuting it into other satisfactions was through trade. Too much of anything is too much.

The market place serves not only to diffuse the abundances that human specialization makes possible, but it is also a distributor of the munificences of nature. For, in her inscrutable way, nature has spread the raw materials by which humans live over the face of the globe; and unless some way were devised for distributing these raw materials, they would serve no human purpose. Thus, through the conduit of trade the fish of the sea reach the miner's table and fuel from the inland mine or well reaches the boiler of the fishing boat; tropical fruits are made available to northerners, whose iron mines, in the shape of tools, make production easier in the tropics. It is by trade that the far-flung warehouses of nature are made accessible to all the peoples of the world and life on this planet becomes that much more enjoyable.

We think of trade as the barter of tangible things simply because that is obvious. But a correlative of the exchange of things is the exchange of ideas, of the knowledge and cultural accumulations of the parties to the transaction. In fact, embodied in the goods is the intelligence of the producers; the excellent woolens imported from England carry evidence of thought that has been given to the art of weaving, and Japanese silks arouse curiosity as to the ideas that went into their fabrication. We acquire knowledge of people through the goods we get from them. Aside from that correlative of trade, there is the fact that trading involves human contacts: and when humans meet, either physically or by means of communication, ideas are exchanged. "Visiting" is the oil that lubricates every market place operation.

It was only after Cuba and the Phillippines were drawn into our trading orbit that interest in the Spanish language and customs was enlivened, and the interest increased in proportion to the volume of our trade with South America. As a consequence, Americans of the present generation are as familiar with Spanish dancing and music as their forefathers, under the influence of commercial contacts with Europe, were at home with the French minuet and the Viennese waltz. When ships started coming from Japan, they brought with them stories of an interesting people, stories that enriched our literature, broadened our art concepts, and added to our operatic repertoire.

It is not only that trading in itself necessitates some understanding of the customs of the people one trades with, but that the cargoes have a way of arousing curiosity as to their source, and ships laden with goods are followed with others carrying explorers of ideas; the open port is a magnet for the curious. So, the tendency of trade is to break down the narrowness of provincialism, to liquidate the mistrust of ignorance. Society, then, in its most comprehensive sense, includes all who for the improvement of their several circumstances engage in trade with one another; its ideational character tends toward a blend of the heterogeneous cultures of the traders. The market place unifies Society.

The concentration of population determines the character of Society only because contiguity facilitates exchange. But contiguity is a relative matter, depending on the means for making contacts; the neutralization of time and space by mechanical means makes the whole world contiguous. The isolationism that breeds an ingrown culture, and a mistrust of outside cultures, melts away as faster ships, faster trains, and faster planes bring goods and ideas from the great beyond. The perimeter of Society is not fixed by political frontiers but by the radius of its commercial contacts. All people who trade with one another are by that very act brought into community.

The Strategy of War

The point is emphasized by the strategy of war. The first objective of a general staff is to destroy the market place mechanisms of the enemy; the destruction of his army is only incidental to that purpose. The army could well enough be left intact if his internal means of communication were destroyed, his ports of entry immobilized, so that specialized production, which depends on trade, could no longer be carried on; the people, reduced to primitive existence, thus lose the will to war and sue for peace. That is the general pattern of all wars. The more highly integrated the economy the stronger will be the nation in war, simply because of its ability to produce an abundance of both military implements and economic goods; on the other hand, if its ability to produce is destroyed, if the flow of goods is interrupted, the more susceptible to defeat it is, because its people, unaccustomed as they are to primitive conditions, are the more easily discouraged. There is no point to the argument as to whether "guns" or "butter" are more important in the prosecution of war.

It follows that any interference with the operation of the market place, however done, is analogous to an act of war. A tariff is such an act. When we are "protected" against Argentine beef, the effect (as intended) is to make beef harder to get, and that is exactly what an invading army would do. Since the duty does not diminish our desire for beef, we are compelled by the diminished supply to put out more labor to satisfy that desire; our range of possibilities is foreshortened, for we are faced with the choice of getting along with less beef or abstaining from the enjoyment of some other good. The absence of a plenitude of meat from the market place lowers the purchasing power of our labor. We are poorer, even as is a nation whose ports have been blockaded.

Moreover, since every buyer is a seller, and vice versa, the prohibition against their beef makes it difficult for Argentineans to buy our automobiles and this expression of our skills is constricted. The effect of a tariff is to drive a potential buyer out of the market place. The argument that "protection" provides jobs is patently fallacious. It is the consumer who gives the worker a job, and the consumer who is prevented from consuming might as well be dead, as far as providing productive employment.

Incidentally, is it jobs we want, or is it beef? Our instinct is to get the most out of life with the least expenditure of labor. We labor only because we want; the opportunity to produce is not a boon, it is a necessity. Neither the domestic nor the foreign producer "dumps" anything into our laps. There is a price on everything we want and the price is always the weariness of toil. Whatever causes us to put out more toil to acquire a given amount or kind of satisfactions is undesirable, for it conflicts with our natural urge for a more abundant life. Such is a tariff, an embargo, an import quota or the modern device of raising the price of foreign goods by arbitrarily lowering the value of our money. Any restriction of trade, internal or external, does violence to a man's primordial drive to improve his circumstances.

Effects of Barriers

Just as trade brings people together, tending to minimize cultural differences, and makes for mutual understanding, so do impediments to trade have the opposite effect. If the customer is always "right," it is easy to assume that there is something wrong with the non-buyer. The faults of those who refuse to do business with us are accentuated not only by our loss but also by the sting of personal affront. Should the boy with the tops refuse to trade with the boy who has marbles, they can no longer play together; and this desocialization can easily stir up an argument over the relative demerits of their dogs or parents. Just so, for all our protestations of good neighborliness, the Argentinean has his doubts about our intentions when we bolt our commercial doors against him; compelled to look elsewhere for more substantial friendship, he is inclined to think less of our national character and culture.

The by-product of trade isolationism is the feeling that the "outsider" is a "different kind" of person, and therefore inferior, with whom social contact is at least undesirable if not dangerous. To what extent this segregation of people by trade restrictions is the cause of war is a moot question, but there can be no doubt that such restrictions are irritants that can give other causes for war more plausibility; it makes no sense to attack a good customer, one who buys as much of our products as he can use and pays his bills regularly. Perhaps the removal of trade restrictions throughout the world would do more for the cause of universal peace than can any political union of peoples separated by trade barriers; indeed, can there be a viable political union while these barriers exist? And, if freedom of trade were the universal practice, would a political union be necessary?

The Spurious Logic of Protectionism

Let us test the claims of "protectionists" with an experiment in logic. If a people prosper by the amount of foreign goods they are not permitted to have, then a complete embargo, rather than a restriction, would do them the most good. Continuing that line of reasoning, would it not be better all around if each community were hermetically sealed off from its neighbor, like Philadelphia from New York? Better still, would not every household have more on its table if it were compelled to live on its own production? Silly as this *reductio ad absurdum* is, it is no sillier than the "protectionist" argument that a nation is enriched by the amount of foreign goods it keeps out of its market, or the "balance of trade" argument that a nation prospers by the excess of its exports over imports.

Yet, if we detach ourselves mentally from entrenched myths, we see that acts of internal isolationism such as described in our syllogism are not infrequent. A notorious instance of this is the French *octroi*, a tax levied on products entering one district from another. Under cover of "quarantine" regulations, Florida and California have mutually excluded citrus fruits grown in the other state. Labor unions are violent advocates of opulence-through-scarcity, as when they restrict, by direct violence or by laws they have had enacted, the importation of materials made outside their jurisdiction. A tax on trucks entering one state from another is of a piece with this line of reasoning. Thus, the "protectionist" theory of fence-building is internalized, and in the light of these facts our *reductio ad absurdum* is not so farfetched. The market place, of course, scoffs at such scarcity-making measures, for it yields no more than it receives; if its offerings are made scarce by trade restrictions, that which remains becomes harder to get, calls for an expenditure of more labor to acquire. The wage-level of Society is lowered.

The myth of "protectionism" rests on the notion that the be-all and end-all of human life is laboring, not consumption—and certainly not leisure. If that were so, then the slaves who built pyramids were most ideally situated; they worked much and received little. Likewise, the Russians chained to "five year plans" have achieved heaven on earth, and so did the workers who, during the depression, were put to moving dirt from one side of the road to the other. Extending this notion that exertion for the sake of exertion is the way to prosperity, then a people would be most prosperous if they all labored on projects with no reference to their individual sense of value. What is euphemistically called "war production" is a case in point; there is in fact no such thing, since the purpose of production is consumption; and it is not on record that any worker built a battleship because he wanted it and proved his craving by willingly giving up anything in exchange for it. Keeping in mind the exaltation of laboring, would not a people be most uplifted if all of them were set to building battleships, nothing else, in return for the necessaries that would enable them to keep building battleships? They certainly would not be unemployed.

Yet, if we base our thinking on the natural urge of the individual to better his circumstances and widen his horizon, operating always under the natural law of parsimony (the most for the least effort), we are compelled to the conclusion that effort which does not add to the abundance of the market place is useless effort. Society thrives on trade simply because trade makes specialization possible, specialization increases output, and increased output reduces the cost in toil for the satisfactions men live by. That being so, the market place is a most humane institution.

2

Serving Consumers
by W. M. Curtiss

Today, major news magazines remind us that the Smoot-Hawley Tariff Act exacerbated and prolonged the Great Depression, and middle-of-the-road columnists take free trade for granted as an ideal. It may be hard, therefore, to realize what a pioneer W. M. Curtiss was in his insistence that The Foundation for Economic Education must support free trade. Dr. Curtiss (1904–1979) was a member of the staff at FEE from its beginnings in 1946 until 1973, serving as Executive Secretary and as Director of FEE Seminars and also initiating and directing FEE's College-Business Exchange Program. His monograph, The Tariff Idea, *published by FEE in 1953, was one of the first contemporary books to present the economic, political, and moral case for free trade as the path to peace for individuals and nations, at a time when support of such a policy lost FEE many potential donations from businessmen.*

The article presented here first appeared in The Freeman *in May 1964, and foreshadows many themes that are treated in more detail elsewhere in this book. It also uniquely emphasizes the moral importance of property rights as a basis for policy and the scope for consumer interests and consumer decisions that economic liberty provides.*

Trade between one person and another probably has been going on as long as man had something he could call his own. In a peaceful society, two neighbors compare their respective supplies and wants, and find opportunity to swap to their mutual advantage. That's really all there is to trade—one person giving up something he has for something he wants more. So long as the trade is voluntary and peaceful, both parties think they benefit from the deal. If not, why trade?

Now, it's true, trade gets more complicated when money comes into the picture—and especially so if each trader uses a different kind of money. Distance and time and transportation also complicate the trade. Still further complications arise when there are government licenses to cope with, and import quotas, and exchange quotas, and bilateral agreements, and most-favored-nation agreements, and a host of other restrictions.

The first essential to orderly trade between people is private ownership of property. A man must possess and be able to deliver what he offers.

Just why do people trade one thing for another?

Man attempts to satisfy his desires with the least possible effort—a worthy trait indeed, so long as he does not tread on the equal right of others to do the same. This is the *principle of conservation* as applied to human effort—and it is the basis of all economic progress.

In satisfying his desires, modern man is constantly exchanging goods and services with other men. In making these exchanges, his urge is always to obtain something which he values more highly than what he gives up.

But this trait in man's nature sometimes leads to trouble. Some men think that the easiest way to satisfy their wants is to steal from others. And perhaps this would be so except for one thing: The victims resent it! In most societies, of course, stealing is considered a violation of the basic codes of conduct, ethics, and morality; and, it is a violation of our first assumption, *a person has the right to own property*. If stealing is considered wrong in a society, it is natural that laws be passed to punish thieves.

One of the facts of life that makes trading desirable and useful is that most of the material things we want are always in short supply. There just isn't enough to go around. It is for this reason that things command a price in the market and that persons find it desirable to trade and improve their position.

The material welfare of an individual, a family, a group, or a nation is determined by the amount of goods and services at its disposal. Neither nations nor individuals can consume what they do not have. Thus, the material level of living which the people of a nation enjoy is measured by their production—plus or minus international gifts.

The American family has more material things than has the Chinese or Indian or Russian family because the American worker produces more. The reasons for this greater productivity—capital accumulation, private ownership, tools, and the like—are fairly well known. The point is that high-level consumption is based on high-level production and exchange—on abundance, not on scarcity.

Trade between individuals, of course, would never take place unless each party to the trade expected to benefit from the exchange. When two men voluntarily agree to trade horses, it is certain that each believes he is to get something better than what he is to give up. Why else would either consent to the trade?

There seems to be a general feeling that when money is exchanged for, say, an automobile, it is only the seller of the car who benefits. But doesn't the buyer benefit as well? Doesn't he value the car more than the money he gives up? If not, why does he willingly make the exchange?

Is it any different when the bargaining parties happen to live in different cities? Or in different states? Or in different countries?

Throughout history, and to a dramatic degree in the past one hundred years, men have become specialists. Suppose, for instance, that each person had to produce his own television set. Life just wouldn't be long enough for him to do it. He would have to be an electronics engineer, a mining engineer, a metallurgist, a cabinet-maker, a glass manufacturer, a machine-tool maker—there must be hundreds of skills involved in building a television set.

But while he was mastering the skills necessary to produce his television set, who would provide him with food, clothing, and shelter? And how could he learn of electronics without books and the accumulation of years of research?

Not many decades past, practically every working hour was required just to provide the food, clothing, and shelter necessary to keep alive. Most people were farmers. There was precious little besides the products of the farm available to families, for the simple reason that eight or nine out of every ten families had to work as hard as they could to feed and clothe the ten families. Specialization? Yes, they had it in a limited way. But today (1964) in the United States it requires little more than one family in ten to produce enough food and fiber for all ten families. The other nine families can make television sets, automobiles, household furnishings; they can be teachers, doctors, clergymen, or producers of a host of other goods and services.

Specialization is made possible by what economists call "comparative advantage." We see this clearly in athletic events. Some persons are better than others at throwing a ball or batting a ball or passing a football or playing tennis or running or jumping. They have a comparative advantage and thus are specialists. The same is true of writing a novel, operating a typewriter or a punch press, or treating a disease.

Comparative advantage is sometimes the result of geography. A clear example is the production of bananas. Bananas can be grown under glass in the state of New York—and a few are. Of course, they are very expensive when grown this way. Through the cooperation of nature, bananas are grown at much less cost in Central America. That area, then, has a comparative advantage in the growing of bananas.

In a free, competitive market, the price of a commodity or service depends on what someone is willing to pay for it. So it is with the wages of labor. The employer must be willing to pay if he wants men to work for him. How much he will pay will depend on the labor market and indirectly on how much his workers can produce.

Therefore, we find relatively high wages in a country where the productivity of the workers is high. Where we find an extremely low level of wages, we can be sure that the productivity of the workers is low.

The reason for such a tremendous difference in the production of workers in different countries can be told very briefly in one word, *tools*. Tools include plant and equipment, as well as the actual machines the worker operates. In the United States, it now (1964) requires an average investment of $16,000 to $20,000 to provide one industrial worker with tools. Some modern industrial plants cost as much as $100,000 for each worker employed there. Contrast this with a hoe or wheelbarrow used by a Chinese worker.

The Consumer Reigns

In an economic sense, the only reason for producing anything is to satisfy the desires of consumers. This idea seems simple enough, but it is often lost from sight as an economy becomes more and more complex and specialized. In a subsistence economy, where the producer is also the consumer, production is obviously for consumption. In such an economy, the family is acutely aware that it must produce food in order to eat; to provide its clothing, sheep must be raised or fur-bearing animals hunted. The family is both producer and consumer of everything it has.

The consumer is, in effect, the court of last appeal in a free market. He is the judge who convicts or acquits. He either accepts or rejects the goods and services offered—taking into account his own desires, his buying power, and the alternate products available. He cares not a whit, at the moment, what it may have cost someone to produce the goods.

To ignore these decisions of the consumer is economic suicide—witness the demise each year of business firms which were guilty of ignoring or misjudging the consumer.

So, we know why people trade; we know the importance of specialization and trade in providing people with an increasing amount of the material things they like; and we know that the only reason production and trade take place is to serve the consumer. With this background, let's take a look at some of the road blocks that sometimes get in the way of trade—that prevent a consumer from making the best possible exchange of whatever he has to offer for whatever it is he wants.

Trade Barriers

Years ago, piracy on the high seas was one of the road blocks to trade. Goods that got through had to bear the cost of those that did not. As a result, consumers got less for their money, or whatever it was they traded, than if there had been no piracy.

There are many kinds of road blocks today—most of them thrown up by governments—either in the exporting country or the importing country or both. Tariffs are just one of these road blocks and probably not even the most important at this time. However, tariffs are pretty simple and once one has an understanding of them, other types of restrictions can be more easily understood.

Probably the most common argument in defense of tariffs is that they keep our domestic wages high; that they keep wages in this country from being reduced to the level of wages in the countries from which we import. It is often put this way: "Tariffs protect us against the competition of low-paid foreign labor. If we accept their goods, we must accept their wage levels."

To begin with, we must not lose sight of the reason why wages in this country are higher than in some others. The level of wages depends upon the productivity of the workers. Our workers are highly productive, largely because of the tools with which they work. In countries where there is a limited accumulation of capital, the tools of the workers are limited. Thus, their productivity is low, and so are wages.

The level of living in a nation depends upon the amount of goods and services available for consumption. If certain individuals in a nation voluntarily trade some of their possessions for the products of another country, it follows that what they receive is worth more to them than what they give up. Otherwise, they would not trade. The total value of the goods and services available for consumption is greater after the trade. The level of living has been raised.

Consider, for a moment, a product made entirely by hand labor. Hand embroidery or other needlework will illustrate. Assume that a woman in Italy working for a very low wage can turn out handmade needlework comparable to that produced by an American woman working for a relatively high wage. It is obvious that the Italian product can be sold in this country for less than it would cost to produce it here. Does that mean that if we import the Italian product the American woman's wage will necessarily be reduced to the level of the Italian woman's wage? Not at all. Why is the wage of the American woman high? It is because of the generally high productivity of American labor, which makes it possible for her to get a high wage in an industrial plant, in an office, in a profession, or in some other type of employment.

It is true that, without trade barriers, hand embroidery probably would be imported from Italy. The American producer of hand embroidery, unable to produce and sell a comparable product at a competitive price, would have to turn to producing one of the many products for which a comparative advantage exists. The American producer might, for example, turn to machine production of an article to replace hand embroidery.

This is typical of the readjustments which would be necessitated by a return to free trade. Workers and management alike, having become adjusted to production under tariffs, would have to improve their efficiency or find other outlets for their skills.

Tariffs encourage the production of some things in which the country lacks efficiency and discourage other lines of production in which the country has a comparative advantage. The total value of production, so far as consumers are concerned, is less than it would otherwise be—and this means that real wages are held down by reason of tariffs. So, rather than *protecting* domestic wages generally, tariffs *lower* real wages in all countries affected.

The Unemployment Issue

That is all very well, you may say, but wouldn't a free trade policy lead to unemployment? The prevention of unemployment is one of the usual arguments for tariffs.

This argument is expressed in a number of ways. One is that the removal of a tariff, after an industry has become adjusted to it, will result in unemployment. Another is that by means of tariffs we can put our people to work making the things we now import and thus create employment. Some say: "We do not want such-and-such a country exporting its unemployment to us."

We have observed that if a tariff is removed, a protected industry may be forced out of business by foreign competition. If this happens, the workers in that industry will have to find employment elsewhere. In the embroidery illustration, it is not denied that the existence of the tariff permits some workers to be employed in embroidery manufacturing who would not otherwise be so employed. But what is often lost sight of is that many other job opportunities not now in existence would become available in this country if people could buy the imported embroidery and spend their tariff money as they please. The money which the consumer formerly had to pay for tariffs could be spent to purchase or produce new products or more of existing products or services.

Tariffs turn a country toward self-sufficiency. A farm family might erect such a high tariff wall around its farm that there could be no trade in goods and services with outsiders. Certainly, no one would be unemployed on that farm, but neither would there be the high level of living the family now enjoys. If the tariff wall around the farm were removed, no one would necessarily be disemployed, and the farmer's household would enjoy a vastly higher level of living—and so would outsiders.

The question of employment or unemployment, except for temporary adjustments, has no place in a consideration of tariffs. It would be as logical to argue that the buggy whip industry should have been subsidized in order to keep its workers employed when there no longer was a demand for buggy whips.

The pattern of production within our own country is perhaps the best illustration of how free trade builds a high level of living. Steel is produced in Pittsburgh, automobiles in Detroit, cotton in the South, meat and grain in the Midwest and the Great Plains, shoes in St. Louis, clothing in New England and New York—just to mention a few of the products and areas of specialization.

"Yes," you may say, "but tariffs don't completely shut off trade." True, but they shut off trade to whatever extent they are effective. The effect of a tariff on wool is that we must employ more of our domestic resources in the production of wool than would be necessary if we imported more of it. A tariff on Swiss watches encourages the production of watches in our own country because it prevents their importation at a lower cost. And by keeping prices higher, such tariffs reduce our consumption of wool and watches.

Another argument for tariffs is that new industries cannot survive if they must compete with firmly established industries in other countries. It is said, "Give them a chance to get established, and they can then compete."

History has shown that protection in the form of tariffs imposed to protect infant industries is difficult, if not impossible, to throw off. The protected infant never grows up to attain self-responsibility. And little wonder! In any industry, protected or not, there are firms which are barely able to stay in business—even though other firms in the same industry are operated profitably. If the crutch of tariffs is removed, these marginal producers must either improve their efficiency or go out of business. If they can do the former, why didn't they do it before the crutch was removed?

Those who use the infant-industry argument appear to place emphasis on the virtue of industry, as such, rather than on the goods produced. They seem to be confusing means and ends. We must not lose sight of the fact that *consumption is the sole end and purpose of all production.*

Advantages of Free Trade

The elimination of trade barriers would have three very important beneficial effects:

1. It would permit our economy to gain from the specialization and comparative advantage in production to be found all over the world.

2. It would help the so-called underdeveloped areas of the world to help themselves. It would give them a better chance to produce and trade.

3. It would be the best way to cement friendly relations between Americans and other peoples all over the world. How can one individual become angry with another when they are permitted to trade freely and voluntarily, knowing that both parties to the deal will benefit? In such trade, there is no danger of secret diplomacy, of playing special favorites, of handling other nations as pawns—pitting one against the other to seek a gain or even to attempt a precarious balance.

But what can we do about all these trade restrictions—not only tariffs but all the others? Isn't it a difficult political problem? Of course it is, and it requires political answers—unfortunately. I say unfortunately because, too often, a political solution may not be the best economic solution.

The will to remove restrictions on trade can come about only through understanding—through the realization that restrictions do not yield the benefits claimed for them. Worse than that, they are harmful—harmful economically and harmful to the cause of peace, friendship, and good will, at home and abroad.

On the surface, tariff protection seems to offer benefits to the owners and workers of a protected industry. When a tariff is first applied, the producers of the particular product affected have a price advantage which should be reflected in higher profits. But tariffs do not prohibit domestic competition within an industry. The higher profits attract newcomers to the field, and competition tends to erase the gains from the special privilege. After this happens, the producers are back in their former competitive position. In order to maintain any benefit, they will have to continue to ask for new privileges as the old ones lose their power—much as a drug addict must use more and more of the drug to avoid the suffering it is supposed to relieve.

Thus, the so-called "benefits" of tariff protection are illusory—the only consequence of the tariff being that the domestic owners and workers are competing with one another in an industry erected on a false base. The base is false and weak because it is supported by the threat of force—force which directs individual spending—instead of by voluntary choices. The force is directed against consumers, the friends and neighbors of those who seek special privileges for themselves. But consumers do not respond kindly to force or threats of force. They have only so much buying power, and they cannot be forced to buy more of everything. Nor will they buy a commodity as freely as before if its price is forced upward by a "protective" tariff. Thus, tariffs serve merely to put the whole economy on an artificial foundation instead of on a sound business foundation. No one really gains—and nearly everyone loses—by this arrangement. It stifles progress.

Adjustments such as those which would be required by the removal of tariffs are taking place constantly in a free economy. When the automobile made its appearance, the operators of livery stables and the manufacturers of buggies were inconvenienced. They had to turn to something else. But they soon found themselves benefiting in two ways: First, as consumers, they benefited generally from the automobile; and second, the new job opportunities within the new and expanding automobile industry were more attractive than those in a dying industry. Thus, the removal of trade restrictions would not be as painful as it may at first appear—even to those who think they benefit from them.

To argue that tariffs cannot be removed when an industry or a nation has become adjusted to operating under trade restrictions is no different in principle than to argue against all technological change and advance.

Such arguments indicate, however, that it is politically difficult to remove restrictions once they have become established. Powerful minority interests vigorously withstand changes of this type. "Tariffs should be removed gradually," say some, "in order not to offend too severely those who have a direct interest in the protected industry." This overlooks the persons who have long been offended by not being able to exchange to advantage. It argues that the offense to the consumer may be continued without injustices.

A familiar argument is: "We are willing to give up our protection if all others will give up theirs." As a political argument, this is fairly effective since it is practically impossible to face the combined forces of all minority groups. Economically, of course, the argument has no validity. The way to begin is to begin. The amount of human energy released by the removal of restrictions will be astounding.

Perhaps the greatest obstacle to the removal of trade barriers is the belief expressed by small groups of producers: "Yes, but our case is different; an exception should be granted in just this one instance." Grant a single exception and the floodgates are opened to all sorts of pressure groups. The result will be a continuation of the political chaos which we now find in the area of trade restrictions.

Basically, the issue of tariffs and other trade restrictions is a moral one. This is not to deny that it is also an economic issue. It is merely a matter of emphasis. Unless economic principles are in harmony with good moral principles, they are not good economics.

Government grows strong and dictatorial by the granting of special favors. Trade restrictions are just another of the handouts which a government can grant, thereby increasing its power over individuals—to the detriment of all.

The moral basis for free trade rests on the assumption that an individual has the right to the product of his own labor—stealing is bad because ownership is good. This involves property rights. Property rights are human rights, and to try to distinguish between them is merely to play with words—and on emotions.

The right to own property involves the right to use it, to keep it, to give it away, or to exchange it. Unless this is possible, one does not own property. To lay obstacles in the path of ownership, use, or exchange of property is a violation of the human right to own property.

Fallacy and Fact

Economists from Adam Smith down to the present have quite generally agreed that tariffs are bad economics. And it is not difficult to discover why.

Tariffs and other trade restrictions contribute to scarcity rather than to abundance. We are sometimes fooled by the introduction of money into trade; but basically, it is the abundance of goods and services, widely distributed, that contributes to a high level of material well-being.

There is ample evidence that a high level of living in any country cannot be achieved without a high degree of division of labor—specialization. Rather than a jack-of-all-trades, each person is the master of one. This calls for a high degree of cooperative effort and exchange. Production by this process rests on the principle of comparative advantage—of production where conditions are most favorable.

A fallacy of protectionists is that employment, of itself, is a worthy economic objective. Employment, however, is merely a means to an end—and the end is production for consumption. No doubt employment was high during the building of the Great Wall of China or the Pyramids of Egypt. A dictator can always achieve full employment. Hitler did it in Germany; and we had our leaf-raking projects.

But under freedom—freedom to produce and to trade voluntarily—men will have just as much employment as they desire. Actually, tariffs have nothing to do with employment. Employment can be high or low—with or without such trade restrictions. Tariffs do not create better jobs for individuals. They simply tend to keep people at jobs which are less productive of useful goods and services than they would be under free trade.

Protectionists have claimed that wage levels can be maintained or increased by shutting out imports from areas with low real wages. Wage levels are determined by the productivity of labor. This, in turn is determined by the investment of capital in the tools of production. The products we import are more valuable to us than our exports; otherwise, the trade would not be made. Rather than produce the imported product here, our own labor is released to produce something we are better fitted to produce.

Failure to recognize that satisfaction of desires is the sole purpose and end of production has led protectionists to support tariffs, subsidies, and other measures. Had we consistently followed such a policy, we would now be subsidizing 80 per cent of our population in agricultural pursuits, as well as in the manufacture of buggy whips and candles. Economic progress cannot take place under such a system.

The removal of tariffs restores justice to consumers—to millions and millions of consumers. The fact that it may seem to result in a temporary inconvenience for a few producers is merely the correction of an injustice previously established.

Free trade is such a simple solution for so many of the world's ills. It doesn't require endless hours of debate in the United Nations or the International Labor Organization or the Food and Agriculture Organization, or any other world-wide debating society. It requires only that *one nation* see the light and remove *its* restrictions. The results will be immediate and widespread.

It isn't necessary for all nations to agree jointly and simultaneously to remove restrictions. If only one nation does it, some good is accomplished—both for itself and for its customers. A great nation, such as the United States, could do it and thus set an example for others to follow. It would not be meddling in the affairs of other nations; it would merely be looking after the best interests of its own citizens. And instead of being resentful, other nations would be grateful.

3

Protectionism

by Bettina Bien Greaves

Before we turn to a more specific examination of our subject, we need to place it in context. What is the history of the United States with respect to trade barriers, and what arguments have been raised for and against protectionism? Who better to do this than Bettina Bien Greaves, who since 1951 has been culling and sending out to students and debaters the introductory arguments for economic freedom in every imaginable area of application: water policy, agricultural policy, welfare policy, foreign affairs—you name it—on behalf of The Foundation for Economic Education? Among her published works is a two-volume "do-it-yourself" textbook, Free Market Economics *(published by FEE). Her discussion of protectionism first appeared in* American Trade Policy: The Thirty-Sixth Discussion and Debate Manual, *published in 1962 by Artcraft Press, Columbia, Missouri under the auspices of The Committee on Discussion and Debate of The National University Extension Association, for the use of high school debaters all over the country.*

Once upon a time, the issue was clear cut. Those who favored high tariffs were protectionists; those who opposed them, or at least favored only tariffs for revenue, were free traders. But today the situation is not so simple. Politicians speak against high tariffs and advocate "freer trade" but at the same time, they favor protection in various guises. Few persons, certainly none holding important political positions in this country, consistently advocate true free trade.

When protective tariffs were the principal man-made barriers to international transactions, abolishing them would have meant an immediate improvement in the situation of consumers. Adjustments in production would have had to be made, but the shifts would all tend toward increasing efficiency, greater economy and more consumer satisfaction. Thus the repeal of protective tariffs would, in the long run, have brought higher standards of living to consumers.

Things that could be produced more economically within a country would be made locally, while things that could be had more inexpensively by exchange for domestically-produced goods would be brought from abroad. In a world where protective tariffs were the main artificially-created trade barriers, their repeal would mean that all capital, tools, machines and workers would tend to move into areas and industries where they were most wanted, most useful and productive.

However, the day when protective tariffs were the chief artificial barriers to trade is past. Many other hindrances to trade are now accepted. To usher in free trade simply by abolishing protective tariffs would no longer be possible. Not only protective tariffs but all other protectionist programs—subsidies and trade restrictions of various kinds that help some at the expense of others—must also be abandoned. The whole protectionist philosophy must be rejected. Before we can expect the now-popular protectionism to be abolished, however, widespread understanding of free market principles will have to be developed.

U.S. Tariff History

In this country, tariffs for protection have had a long history. The first bill introduced into the new U.S. House of Representatives, the Tariff Act of 1789, was intended, according to its Preamble, "for the support of the Government, for the discharge of the debts of the United States." But its Preamble also stated that duties should be laid for "the encouragement and protection of manufactures." Nevertheless, the primary purpose of this first tariff law was to produce revenue—and it succeeded. It would have been practically impossible for the new government to rely on taxes collected from a widely scattered people, largely self-sufficient farmers, who were spread far and wide throughout a land with few highways, rivers, or communication lines and who bought and sold comparatively little for money. But it was relatively easy to block highways and harbors at the border, to stop travellers and shippers, and to inspect and tax the things they carried with them. The Founding Fathers believed the United States would have to depend for a long time for its support chiefly on duties on imported articles.[1] As a matter of fact, they did. Until the first income tax was passed during the Civil War, the major share by far of the government's money came every year (except 1814 and 1815) from customs duties.[2]

One of the great debates of the 19th century was over tariffs—for revenue or for protection. Theoretically, there is a difference. A tariff for revenue should not be set so high as to discourage all imports; if it does, it yields no revenue. Custom duties furnish funds only if goods actually cross the border into a country so that the tax can be collected. A tariff for revenue, therefore, is not intended to prevent imports, but rather to tax items consumers want enough to pay more than they would have had to pay in the absence of the import duty. A protective tariff, on the other hand, is designed to discourage imports so as to protect domestic producers from foreign competition. A really effective protective tariff would prevent imports from reaching domestic consumers and thus yield no revenue to the government.

Although a tariff for revenue is not intended to prevent imports, it does raise the price on the domestic market of the imports taxed. And this necessarily affects sales. Some consumers will decide to buy less or not to buy that particular import at all. The tariff is in effect an added cost to importing that gives domestic producers a comparative advantage. Not having to consider that extra cost, domestic producers can spend more to produce the commodity and still afford to sell it at or below the domestic price of the import. As a result, domestic producers may consider producing, or expanding production of, the good concerned when it would not have been worthwhile if the price of the imported commodity had not been artificially raised. Once producers adjust their production and future plans to take this fact into consideration, tariff repeal will hurt them. Tariff repeal would permit importers to lower their selling prices and compete more effectively for consumers. Few producers, whose livelihoods have come to depend on protection, can afford to advocate its repeal.

Although the first duties were not primarily protective, sentiment in favor of using tariff legislation to encourage and protect local manufactures grew. By 1812, protectionism had gained considerable strength. Protectionists and non-protectionists generally split then along state, not political party, lines according to industrial interests. Not until the late 1880's did protection become identified with the Republicans, when they endorsed the high rates later adopted in the McKinley (1890) Tariff Act, while the Democrats under Cleveland sought to lower them.

A significant change in tariff-making took place with the passage of the Tariff Acts of 1922 and 1930, and especially of the Reciprocal Trade Agreements Act (1934). The two earlier laws provided for flexible tariffs, in the attempt to take into account the differences in production costs in the U.S. and abroad. They delegated to the President, with the advice of the Tariff Commission, the power to fix, within certain limits, specific tariffs. The Act of 1934 went still further in giving the President a free hand. He was empowered with considerable latitude to set tariffs, simply by making international agreements with other governments.

Congress continues to relinquish more and more authority in this area to the President and our Executive now requests additional authorities and discretionary powers. This trend represents a move away from free, or even freer trade, and it is a serious threat to democracy and individual freedom. In a recent lecture, Professor Ludwig von Mises, world renowned free market economist, pointed this out: ''A law that gives to the Executive powers which previously were in the jurisdiction of parliamentary choice is a most important first step toward dictatorship.''

Modern Protectionism

The distinction between the two major parties on the basis of tariffs has been dulled in recent decades. Many Republicans still favor high tariffs, and many Democrats lower ones. But the Democratic Party today is certainly not opposed to protection. Both parties have sponsored a whole arsenal of trade restrictions, other than tariffs, which protect domestic producers from foreign competition and otherwise limit goods coming into the country. Quotas, embargoes, ''Buy American'' acts, licensing requirements, quarantines, food and drug standards, anti-dumping laws, and the like, all favor domestic producers to the disadvantage of foreign competitors and consumers. Our government also resorts to subsidies, direct and indirect, to help certain domestic producers and to avoid injury due to foreign imports. Price supports raise farm income; purchases for foreign aid help certain U. S. industries; government stockpiles and domestic produce dumped abroad keep goods off the American market and so help to hold up prices to the benefit of producers.

To be sure, the government's interventions to protect domestic industries have other consequences also. U.S. government gifts and loans to other governments, for instance, may help foreign producers equip factories with new and efficient machinery and put them in a better position to compete in the American market than they would have been without that assistance. U.S. farm price supports encourage some foreign farmers to grow more than they would have otherwise with the hope of selling in the high-priced U.S. market. Our dumping abroad discourages some production. High prices on the U.S. market encourage imports. And the high taxes which U.S. producers must pay to support these and other subsidy programs raise their costs and hurt their competitive position as compared with that of foreign producers. However, neither political party thinks of trying to cure these injustices by repealing the political interventions to permit free and open competition.

The philosophy of protectionism dominates both political parties. Their leading spokesmen believe government should interfere with trade, for they lack confidence that the free and voluntary transactions of private individuals and traders would promote the ''national interest.'' In his message to Congress (January 26, 1962), President Kennedy asked for new tariff bargaining powers ''to maintain the leadership of the free world'' and he spoke of the ''philosophy of the free market—the wider economic choice for men and nations.'' However, he did not ask for completely free trade and outright repeal of protective tariffs. He called instead for broad discretionary presidential power to negotiate with other political powers, to adjust tariff rates and to grant subsidies—to U.S.

companies, farmers and workers "who suffer damage from increased foreign import competition."[3] He requested authority to help those hurt, through special tax relief, technical assistance, vocational education, and even direct financial aid in getting relocated in new enterprises. Protection against imports is no longer simply a matter of high tariffs. Thus, abolishing protective tariffs alone would accomplish relatively little today towards creating a free trade world.

Protection versus Free Trade

The idea of protection and of protective tariffs is popular for several basic reasons. The most common arguments given are that it is in the "national interest" to maintain wages and living standards, protect industries and skills considered vital for defense, preserve domestic markets for domestic producers, and encourage infant industries. Now "protection" can obviously help some producers. But it should never be forgotten that this help is always at the expense of hurting others. Some wages, industries and markets may be artificially maintained at higher levels than if trade were free. If importers had unhampered access to the domestic market, some new industries might not develop, others might decline, certain skills might be lost, certain imported goods sold on the domestic market in preference to domestically-produced commodities. And if sales of domestic production dropped because consumers preferred the imports, some workers might have to look for different kinds of work at lower wages. But would it be in the "national interest" to prevent these changes? Should they be avoided at the cost of making all consumers pay higher prices for the things they buy?[4]

There is truth in the arguments that protection will help some producers temporarily, but it cannot do this without hurting others. Advocates of protection ignore the fundamental reason trades are made in the first place. They neglect the basic truth that, when two parties decide of their own free choice to exchange what each has with one another, both expect to gain. Each considers what he will be giving up less valuable to him than what he expects to get in return. The two parties to any voluntary transaction always have different views with respect to the relative values of the particular items being traded. Persons may barter (exchange goods and services directly), buy (exchange money for goods and services), or sell (exchange goods and services for money); but in every instance, when the decision is voluntary, each person hopes to be better off as a result of the trade or exchange. If either one did not think so, he would refuse to make the exchange and no trade would take place.

Both parties to any trade always value what they will receive more highly, under the circumstances, than what they are giving up. Think about this for a while. When you buy a suit or dress, a movie ticket, LP record, ice cream soda, a bag of groceries or a book, don't you want that more than the money you give to the clerk? If not, you keep your money until you find something else which you want more than you do the money you pay for it. Of course, you may make a mistake and think you want something, only to decide later you were wrong. But when you buy you always expect to gain. Your purchase represents a gain for the seller too, for he has a different viewpoint, he wants your money more than the thing you are buying. Just as you could refuse to buy, he can refuse to sell if he does not value your money more than what he is selling.

This is the basis of all voluntary transactions—between individuals and business firms within a community, as well as between individuals and business firms from different nations. You buy things because you want them more than what they cost. International traders do the same. They prefer oil from Arabia, coffee from Brazil, newsprint from Canada, for instance, to the price they must pay for them. The buyer may want to use these things himself. More often in the field of international trade, he expects to resell them, refine them, or use them in manufactures in the hope of finding potential buyers who will place a higher value on having them at that time and place and will, therefore, be willing to pay more than their total cost to him.

Voluntary Transactions Make Production Easier

Ever since the Lord told Adam, "In the sweat of thy face shalt thou eat bread" and put him, with Eve, out of the Garden of Eden "to till the ground," people have had to work for their living. The supply of the things men want is limited. So is man's time and energy. Yet human wants are many. Therefore, everybody wants to use what he has in the way of natural resources, time, energy and tools as wisely and as economically as he can. Any instrument, idea, or means that permits a person to get more for less cost is a help toward greater wealth. The discovery that he could gain by trading with other persons was a tremendous step in that direction.

Individuals recognized the advantages of trading in the early ages of mankind—of course, more or less subconsciously at first. For some time it was thought that the seller of goods and services who received money for his labors was the only gainer. But one early author recognized as long ago as 1701 that the spender of money also gained:

> The true and principal Riches, whether of private Persons, or of whole Nations, are Meat, and Bread, and Cloaths, and Houses, the Conveniences as well as Necessaries of Life; the several Refinements and Improvements of these, the secure Possession and Enjoyment of them. These for their own sakes, Money, because 'twill purchase these, are to be esteemed Riches. . . . To exchange Bullion [gold and silver] for Indian Manufactures, is to exchange the same for Manufactures more valuable than the

Manufactures which were exported to procure, and are equivalent to so much Bullion: is to exchange the same for Manufactures which may themselves be exchang'd for more Bullion; is to exchange the secondary, for more of the principal Riches than are elsewhere to be had upon the same Terms: And therefore it is sufficiently prov'd, that the Exchange of Bullion for Indian Manufactures, is an Exchange of less for greater value.[5]

As this pioneer economist explained, people import goods from other countries for the same reason you and I buy things at a store—because it is cheaper and easier than producing them in our homes. Most people in this country today buy food from a store; they can get more to eat, cheaper and with less work, by doing something else—for instance, by driving a truck, working in a factory, teaching school, selling real estate, nursing or doctoring, than they could by growing and processing their own food. For the same reason, traders buy coffee in Brazil, oil in Arabia, newsprint in Canada, and so on. They can get more for less. Similarly, Brazilians, Arabians and Canadians find it easier and cheaper to get cotton fiber, automobiles, and chemicals by producing coffee, oil and newsprint to exchange.

Ludwig von Mises presents the advantages of trading succinctly in the following quotation from his weighty treatise on economics, *Human Action*:

The inhabitants of the Swiss Jura prefer to manufacture watches instead of growing wheat. Watchmaking is for them the cheapest way to acquire wheat. On the other hand the growing of wheat is the cheapest way for the Canadian farmer to acquire watches. The fact that the inhabitants of the Jura do not grow wheat and the Canadians do not manufacture watches is not more worthy of notice than the fact that tailors do not make their shoes and shoemakers do not make their clothes.[6]

Obstacles to Trade Make Production Harder

Trading makes it possible for each person to get things that are difficult or impossible for him to produce for himself by specializing in what he can do easiest and best. In a simple economy, it was easy to see that this helped everyone concerned, that it would not be sensible to prevent or hinder two persons in any way from making a trade when both of them wanted to. If no trade took place, both would suffer. If the trade were permitted but made more difficult, one or both persons would have had to work a little harder or longer to overcome the obstacle in the path of the transaction.

Taxes on transactions, tariffs or custom duties are obstacles to trade; they make transactions more difficult or more expensive for one or both parties. They may in fact be decisive in preventing a trade entirely. They hinder persons from getting the things they want as cheaply and as simply as possible. They make people work a little longer or harder than they would have had to otherwise to get things through trade, to produce things themselves, to get along with less or to go without some things entirely which they might otherwise have enjoyed. Sellers as well as buyers suffer. Barriers to trade force people to work the same for less return, to work harder or longer for the same return, to work at other skills or trades than those they would have chosen, or get along without some things entirely. They prevent producers from using their time, energy, tools and other resources in the most efficient, economic and effective ways. As a result, consumers can have less for their labor or money. This means that trade barriers reduce total consumer satisfaction. All in all, they reduce the total wealth in the economy.

Trade barriers affect both consumers and producers. Because they raise the selling prices of some goods, consumers may find they cannot afford commodities they would have bought if trade were free. Consumers then must forego their first preferences and be satisfied with second or third choices. Producers shift to supplying less-desired wants and the whole pattern of production changes. Resources are channelled into less economic uses so that fewer things consumers want most can be produced and these fewer things tend to be more costly. In *The Tariff Idea,* W. M. Curtiss of the Foundation for Economic Education pointed out how trade barriers raise economic costs and lower living standards:

> People are more productive when they are free to specialize and to trade—when they are free to accumulate capital with which tools can be provided for the specialized workers. . . . The effect of a tariff on wool is that we must employ more of our domestic resources in the production of wool than would be necessary if we imported it. A tariff on Swiss watches encourages the production of watches in our own country because it prevents their importation at a lower cost. And by keeping prices higher, such tariffs reduce our consumption of wool and watches.
>
> We could raise a tariff barrier against the importation of bananas. If it were high enough, producers in this country would, no doubt, find it possible to grow a few bananas under glass to sell at very high prices to a small market. The level of living, so far as bananas contribute to it, would be decidedly reduced. . . . The workers drawn into banana production would be taken from other occupations more naturally suited to this country—more productive by the measure of a free market. And everyone's level of living would be reduced.[7]

Protection is not in the National Interest

Some persons admit that trade barriers may lead to inefficiencies and more costly production in the short run, redirect production into different patterns from those consumers would have signaled by their voluntary purchases and refusals to purchase under free trade. Yes, they say, custom duties and trade restrictions may discourage imports, but this is not necessarily bad. As a matter of fact, trade barriers should be used to do just that. In their opinion, American markets should be preserved for American producers, American jobs, wages and living standards protected. When imports are limited, domestic producers encounter less competition on the domestic market and, as a result, can sell more of their production at higher prices. This, they claim, serves the "national interest."

Every nation wants economic strength and maximum productive power. These are the goals of the men who erect artificial trade barriers. They believe the stimulus such restrictions give to local industries will more than offset losses from reduced voluntary transactions. If consumers are not able to buy imports, they will purchase domestic products and thus encourage domestic industry and increased national self-sufficiency. Why ship wealth earned within a nation beyond its borders? Why enrich foreigners when that wealth could benefit fellow nationals?

Persons who argue in this vein put things the wrong way around. Trade does not help one party at the expense of the other; trade helps both participants; as a result of trading, both parties are able to get things that they want in the easiest and cheapest way possible. Anything which hinders voluntary transactions, therefore, hurts everyone concerned, makes people work longer, harder or get along with less. Reducing imports thus hurts not only the foreign sellers but also those here at home. As Percy L. Greaves, Jr., free market economist, says:

> Every curb on imports is also a curb on exports, for imports are primarily a payment for exports. Any barrier placed in the way of foreign trade reduces living standards because it reduces the advantages that can be gained from the greater international division of labor, whereby goods are produced by those best able to produce them at the least expense to mankind. Any rise in domestic prices as a result of government intervention also leads to a decrease in foreign trade and the advantages to be gained therefrom. . . . The only true solution to our problems is a world of peaceful free trade with political privileges for none. Every step in that direction is an improvement. Every new intervention makes matters worse.[8]

The protectionists are correct in saying that every consumer in the country will benefit from promoting economic strength and maximum productive power, and that this is in the "national interest." The way to accomplish this desired end, however, is not to reduce the number of voluntary transactions by putting artificial obstacles in the path of trade by subsidizing inefficiency and protecting high costs and wages. The secret lies in leaving the doors open to permit voluntary transactions among all persons who want to trade.

As pointed out above, free trade leaves prices flexible to reflect new consumer demands, encourages industry to be alert and energetic in the constant attempt to improve on its competition, and, in the long run, improves the situation for everybody by encouraging the greatest production possible of the things people want most.

The true source of economic strength and productive power is free trade. A free market is the economic system which best encourages a flexible and vital industrial establishment. The most effective way for a nation to be prepared for whatever eventualities the future may bring is simply to permit voluntary transactions.

In the 19th century, during the great debate on tariffs, William Graham Sumner, then Professor of Political and Social Science at Yale University, discussed this thesis. A dreadful conflict had recently ended between two great powers—one, the North, considerably larger in area, wealth and population than the other, more highly industrialized, its industry having enjoyed the "benefits" of protection for several decades, the other, the South, largely agricultural and "undeveloped." Bettors would have given good odds on a quick victory by the manufacturing North over the "undeveloped" South. Yet, see what Professor Sumner had to say:

The case of the South during the late war is a most striking proof of the fallacy of the "independence" [through protection] doctrine. The South had less of this artificial independence than any country in the world. It was blockaded and inclosed by an immensely superior force, and what happened? First, people found that when they had put their last stake on war, they could do without thousands of things which had seemed essential; second, they found substitutes and makeshifts to take the place of real essentials; third, they found that, so long as they had commodities to exchange which the rest of the world wanted, no power could prevent the exchange from going on. It does not become those who needed four years to subdue the South to argue that it was weak for lack of industrial independence. Indeed, the argument is incomplete in two or three important points. Suppose that the South had not been weakened by slavery; suppose that it had been an independent nation before and had enjoyed free trade, so that its people had possessed all the wealth they might have accumulated; suppose that its enemy had been obliged to seek it over the ocean, and by sea attack only; on such a hypothesis who can believe that the South would have suffered because it had not "enjoyed protection," and who can urge us, on the chances of ever finding ourselves in the position of the South, to go on creating an artificial independence? Our independence lies in union, good government, and free industry. . . . Independent men are those who have wealth, not those whose houses are stored for a siege. Independent nations are those which are wealthy because they can command what they want when they want it. Those will be wealthiest which give industry its freest course in time of peace.[9]

An End to Protectionism

The philosophy of protection now pervades almost every aspect of economic life. Government policy is intent on artificially holding up prices and wages. Custom duties are only one form of protection and their elimination alone would accomplish little or nothing toward solving the real problem. Given the popular sentiment in favor of government intervention, it is unrealistic to expect politicians to permit injury to domestic producers by repeal of tariffs. So long as the protectionist philosophy prevails as strongly as it does today, political pressures would be exerted for the enactment of some new form of protection to take their place, and Congress would continue to provide subsidies of one kind or another in the attempt to retain the economic *status quo* and prevent readjustments to economic reality.

If, however, Congress should be prevailed upon to abolish protective tariffs, with complete recognition of their true economic meaning, this would signal an expansion in the understanding of free market principles. In that event, protective tariffs would not fall alone. With growing appreciation of the advantages to be gained from free trade and flexible markets, not only for the production of consumption goods but also for the creation of an economically strong and wealthy economy, pressure would grow for repeal of all other protectionist programs as well.

> The acme of the policies of all self-styled progressive parties and governments is to raise artificially the prices of vital commodities above the height they would have attained on the markets of unhampered laissez-faire capitalism. . . . The immense majority of the American voters are buyers and consumers, not producers and sellers of sugar. Nonetheless the American Government is firmly committed to a policy of high sugar prices by rigorously restricting both the importation of sugar from abroad and domestic production. Similar policies are adopted with regard to the prices of bread, meat, butter, eggs, potatoes, cotton and many other agricultural products. . . . Things are hardly different in other fields. . . .
>
> Nobody knows today whether he wins more from those policies which are favoring the group to which he himself belongs than he loses on account of the policies which favor all the other groups. But it is certain that all are

adversely affected by the general drop in the productivity of industrial effort and output which these allegedly beneficial policies inevitably bring about. . . .

Conditions being such, the prospects for a genuinely liberal revival may appear propitious. At least fifty per cent of the voters are women, most of them housewives or prospective housewives. . . . They will certainly cast their ballot for candidates who proclaim: Do away peremptorily with all policies and measures destined to enhance prices above the height of the unhampered market! Do away with all this dismal stuff of price supports, parity prices, tariffs and quotas, intergovernmental commodity control agreements and so on! Abstain from increasing the quantity of money in circulation and from credit expansion, from all illusory attempts to lower the rate of interest and from deficit spending! What we want is low prices. In the end these judicious householders will even succeed in convincing their husbands.[10]

Everybody is hurt by government policies which try to protect high prices for producers. Many people already realize that high money wages do not necessarily mean high real wages and they are critical of some government policies. Few persons recognize, however, that the first step must be a complete change in the whole philosophy of government, a thorough rejection of the idea of protectionism in whatever form it takes. This revolution in thinking must start with the thinkers, philosophers, teachers and writers. Discontent with present programs could be turned toward recognition of the economic fallacies behind them. Then protective tariffs would be abolished and with them also all other artificial props to the economy. That would bring the end to protectionism.

1. *The Federalist*, No. 12.

2. *Historical Statistics of the United States (1789–1945): A Supplement to the Statistical Abstract*. U.S. Department of Commerce, Bureau of the Census, 1949.

3. At this writing, Congress is considering legislation to take the place of the Trade Agreements Act, its last extension due to expire June 30, 1962. If the President's suggestions for direct and indirect financial aid to domestic producers hurt by foreign competition are not adopted, some protective devices such as the Peril Point provision for increasing tariffs and the Escape clause will undoubtedly be continued.

4. More than a century ago, the French economist, statesman and author, Frederic Bastiat, answered this question in simple, everyday language. See "The Candlemaker's Petition: and Other Tales" (Irvington-on-Hudson: Foundation for Economic Education).

5. "Considerations on the East-India Trade" (1701), in *Early English Tracts on Commerce*, edited by J. R. McCulloch (London: Cambridge University Press, 1954). pp. 558–559.

6. Ludwig von Mises. *Human Action* (New Haven: Yale University Press, 1949), p. 392.

7. W. M. Curtiss. *The Tariff Idea* (Irvington-on-Hudson, New York: The Foundation for Economic Education, 1953), pp. 47–48.

8. Percy L. Greaves, Jr. "The Welfare State is a Warfare State, II" *Christian Economics* (September 18, 1956).

9. William Graham Sumner. *Lectures on the History of Protection in the United States* (New York: G.P. Putnam's Sons, 1888), p. 38.

10. Ludwig von Mises. "The Political Chances of Genuine Liberalism," in *Planning for Freedom* (South Holland, Illinois: Libertarian Press, 1952), pp. 172–174.

4

Domination through Industrial Superiority

by Frederic Bastiat

Free trade was the concrete policy question that led many British and European thinkers of the early modern period to formulate economic philosophies. As a reminder of this rich heritage, here is a little-known essay by Frederic Bastiat (1801–1850), whose book The Law *has introduced so many readers to the ideas of classical liberalism. Bastiat, who helped to found the first French free-trade association, was a friend and admirer of Richard Cobden of the British Anti-Corn-Law League and translated many of his speeches and articles into French. Free trade was not a narrow issue for these men; it was seen as fundamental to a free society. As Bastiat wrote to Cobden toward the end of the 1840s, "Rather than the fact of free trade alone, I desire for my country the general philosophy of free trade. While free trade itself will bring more material wealth to us, the acceptance of the general philosophy that underlies free trade will inspire all needed reforms."*

This essay was first published in a weekly free-trade newspaper edited by Bastiat, in 1847, but it is as good a demolition of the central argument of economic nationalism—that free trade makes a country "dependent" on those nations from whom it imports—as anything that has been written since. Yet unfortunately, this argument continues to be accepted without examination. (The translation is by Arthur Goddard, in an edition of the essays Economic Sophisms *first published by the D. Van Nostrand Company in 1964 and currently published in paperback by FEE.)*

❝ Just as, in time of war, a nation attains ascendancy over its enemies by virtue of its superiority in weapons, can a nation, in time of peace, attain ascendancy over its competitors by virtue of its industrial superiority?"

This is a question of the highest interest in an age when no one seems to doubt that in the field of industry, as on the field of battle, *the stronger crushes the weaker*.

For this to be so, someone must have discovered, between the labor that is exerted upon things and the violence that is exerted upon men, a melancholy and discouraging analogy; for how could these two kinds of operations be identical in their effects if they are opposite in nature?

And if it is true that in industry, as in war, ascendancy is the necessary result of superiority, why do we concern ourselves with progress or with political economy, since we live in a world in which everything has been so arranged by Providence that one and the same effect—oppression—inevitably follows from principles that are directly opposed to each other?

In regard to the entirely new policy into which free trade is leading England, many people are making the following objection, which, I must admit, carries weight even with the most open-minded among us: Is England doing anything else than pursuing the same end by different means? Has she not always aspired to world supremacy? Assured of superiority in capital and labor, is she not inviting free competition in order to stifle Continental industry, reign supreme, and win for herself the privilege of feeding and clothing the nations she has ruined?

It would be easy for me to demonstrate that these alarms have no basis in fact; that our supposed inferiority is greatly exaggerated; that every one of our major industries is not only holding its ground, but is actually expanding under the impact of foreign competition, and that its inevitable effect is to bring about a general increase in consumption that is capable of absorbing both domestic and foreign products.

Today I propose, rather, to make a frontal attack upon this objection, allowing it all the strength and the advantage of the ground it has chosen. Disregarding for the moment the special case of the English and the French, I shall seek to discover, in general terms, whether a country that, by its superiority in one branch of industry, succeeds in eliminating foreign competition in that industry, has thereby taken a step toward domination over the other country, and the latter a step toward dependence on it; whether, in other words, both do not profit from the operation, and whether it is not the nation that has been bested in this commercial rivalry that profits the most.

If a product is viewed only as *an opportunity for expending labor*, the alarms of the protectionists are certainly well founded. If we consider iron, for example, only in connection with iron-masters, we might well fear that the competition of a country in which iron is a gratuitous gift of Nature could extinguish the fires in the blast furnaces of another country in which there is a scarcity of ore and fuel.

But is this a complete view of the subject? Is iron connected only with those who make it? Does it have no connection with those who use it? Is its sole and ultimate end simply to be produced? And if it is useful, not on account of the labor for which it provides employment, but by reason of the qualities it possesses, the numerous services for which its hardness and its malleability render it fit, does it not follow that a foreigner cannot reduce its price, even to the point of rendering its production in our country completely unprofitable, without doing us more good in the latter respect than harm in the former?

It should be kept in mind that there are many things that foreigners, on account of the natural advantages by which they are surrounded, prevent us from producing directly, and with relation to which we are situated, *in fact*, in the hypothetical position we have been considering with regard to iron. We produce at home neither tea, coffee, gold, nor silver. Does this mean that our industry as a whole thereby suffers some diminution? No; it means only that, in order to create the equivalent value needed to acquire these commodities by way of exchange, we employ *less* labor than would be required to produce them ourselves. We thus have more labor left over to devote to satisfying other wants. We are that much richer and stronger. All that foreign competition has been able to do, even in cases in which it has absolutely eliminated us from a particular branch of industry, is to save labor and increase our productive capacity. Is this the way for the foreigner to attain *mastery* over us?

If someone found a gold mine in France, it does not follow that it would be to our interest to work it. In fact, it is certain that the enterprise should not be undertaken if each ounce of gold absorbed more of our labor than would an ounce of gold bought from Mexico with cloth. In that case it would be better to continue to regard our looms as gold mines. And what is true of gold is no less true of iron.

Saving Labor Strengthens Society

The illusion has its source in our failure to see that foreign superiority eliminates the need for but one particular kind of labor in the domestic market and renders that particular kind of labor superfluous only by putting at our disposal the result of the very labor so eliminated. If men lived in diving bells under water and had to provide themselves with air by means of a pump, this would be an immense source of employment for them. To do anything that might interfere with their employing their labor in this way, *while leaving their conditions unchanged*, would be to inflict frightful harm on them. But if their labor ceases only because there is no longer a need for it, because the men are placed in another environment in which air is introduced into their lungs without effort, then the loss of this labor is in no way regrettable, except in the eyes of those who persist in seeing the sole value of labor in the labor itself.

It is precisely this type of labor that machinery, free trade, and progress of every kind are gradually eliminating; not productive labor, but labor that has become superfluous, surplus labor devoid of purpose or result. Protectionism, on the contrary, puts it back to work; it places us once again under water, in order to furnish us with the opportunity of using the air pump; it compels us to seek for gold in the inaccessible domestic mine rather than in our domestic looms. Its whole effect is expressed in the phrase: *waste of energy*.

It will be understood that I am speaking here of general effects, and not of the temporary inconveniences occasioned by the transition from a bad system to a good one. A momentary disturbance necessarily accompanies every advance. This may be a reason for easing the transition as much as possible; it is not a reason for systematically prohibiting all progress, still less for failing to recognize it.

War Overcomes; Trade Sustains

Industrial competition is generally represented as a conflict; but this is not a true picture of it, or it is true only if we confine ourselves to the consideration of each industry in terms of its effects upon another, similar industry, isolating both of them, in thought, from the rest of mankind. But there is something else to be considered: their effects upon consumption and upon general well-being.

That is why it is not permissible to compare commercial relations, as is often done, to war and to treat the two of them as analogous.

In war, *the stronger overcomes the weaker*.

In business, *the stronger imparts strength to the weaker*. This utterly destroys the analogy.

The English may be strong and skillful; they may have enormous *amortized* investments; they may have at their disposal the two great forces of production: iron and fuel; all this means that the products of their labor are *cheap*. And who profits from the low cost of a product? The person who buys it.

It is not within the power of the English to annihilate absolutely any part whatsoever of our labor. All they can do is to render it superfluous with respect to a given result that has already been achieved, to furnish us the air and at the same time dispense with the pump, to increase thereby the productive capacities at our disposal, and—what is especially noteworthy— to render their alleged ascendancy over us the less possible the more their industrial superiority becomes incontestable.

Thus, by a rigorous yet reassuring demonstration, we reach the conclusion that *labor* and *violence*, which are so opposite in nature, are none the less so in their effects, whatever protectionists and socialists may say of them.

In order to reach this conclusion all that we have to do is to distinguish between labor that has been *abolished* and labor that has been *saved*.

To have less iron *because* one works less, and to have more iron *although* one works less, are things that are more than just different; they are opposite. The protectionists confuse them; we do not. That is all.

We should realize that if the English undertake enterprises that involve a great deal of activity, labor, capital, and intelligence, and a great number of natural resources, it is not just for show, but to procure for themselves a great number of satisfactions in exchange for their products. They certainly expect to receive at least as much as they give, and *what they produce in their own country pays for what they buy elsewhere.* If, therefore, they flood us with their products, it is because they expect to be flooded with ours. In that case, the best way to acquire for ourselves as many of their products as possible is to be free to choose between these two means of obtaining them: direct production or indirect production. All the arts of British Machiavellism cannot force us to make a poor choice.

Let us, then, cease this childish practice of comparing industrial competition to war; whatever element of plausibility this faulty analogy has comes of isolating two competing industries in order to determine the effects of their competition. As soon as one introduces into this calculation the effect produced upon the general well-being, the analogy breaks down.

In a battle, he who is killed is utterly destroyed, and the army is so much the weaker. In industry, a factory closes only when what it produced is replaced, *with a surplus besides*, by the whole of domestic industry. Imagine a state of affairs in which, for each man killed in action, two spring from the ground full of strength and energy. If there is a planet where such things happen, war, it must be admitted, is conducted there under conditions so different from those we see down here that it no longer deserves even to be called by the same name.

Now, this is the distinguishing characteristic of what has been so inappropriately called *industrial warfare*.

Let the English and the Belgians lower the price of their iron, if they can; let them keep on lowering it until they send it to us for nothing. They may quite possibly, by this means, extinguish the fire in one of our blast furnaces, i.e., in military parlance, kill one of our soldiers; but I defy them to prevent a thousand other branches of industry from springing up at once, as a *necessary* consequence of this very cheapness, and becoming more profitable than the one that has been killed.

Our conclusion must be, then, that domination through industrial superiority is impossible and self-contradictory, since every superiority that manifests itself in a nation is transformed into low-cost goods and in the end only imparts strength to all other nations. Let us banish from political economy all expressions borrowed from the military vocabulary: *to fight on equal terms, conquer, crush, choke off, be defeated, invasion, tribute.* What do these terms signify? Squeeze them, and nothing comes out. Or rather, what comes out is absurd errors and harmful preconceptions. Such expressions are inimical to international co-operation, hinder the formation of a peaceful, ecumenical, and indissoluble union of the peoples of the world, and retard the progress of mankind.

Part Two

History, Hunger, and Employment

Having sketched in the general arguments against protectionism and for free trade and called into critical question the overall doctrine of economic nationalism, we want to see how these general statements apply to specific instances. Any general principle and policy prescription must be able to show both that it can deal with problem areas and that its analysis accords with the facts of history.

Here we choose two examples that look at the relationship of trade and war in our past. We begin with Clarence B. Carson's extended description of the mercantile policies that ultimately and unintentionally led to the American Revolution. Then William L. Baker draws on the Civil War blockade to illustrate the fallacy of what he calls "the old trade-is-war doctrine."

There is, however, a school of thought that holds that the past is already out-of-date and sheds but a limited light on our unique contemporary problems. Adherents of this point of view might object that, in today's world, free trade would either exploit underdeveloped nations by causing them mass starvation, or exploit developed nations, by causing them mass unemployment. Either prospect would be unacceptable, and its avoidance would be well worth the risk of international hostility that accompanies protectionism. E. C. Pasour, Jr., and Hans F. Sennholz refute these horrendous scenarios for world hunger and industrial unemployment respectively, showing that in both cases it is the prescribed medicine of protectionist measures that is making the patient ill.

5

The Mercantile Impasse

by Clarence B. Carson

Is it policies of protectionism and economic nationalism that lead to war, or war that leads to such policies as a matter of practical necessity? This is the question addressed by Clarence B. Carson in this next selection, which he devotes to an analysis of the circumstances surrounding the American Revolution, and the role that England's mercantilist policies played in that conflict. Dr. Carson, a historian who has authored ten books and more than 500 articles in his long career, details the ways in which British economic policies worked to the detriment of the colonists and inevitably required the taxation that was the precipitating impetus toward revolution. He concludes that the relationship between protectionist policy and conflict was no accident—not only was it so, but it had to be so. "If trade is free," he writes, *"competition is peaceful, but mercantilism shifts the contest into the realm of governmental power. When governments contest for advantage in this way they are moving in the direction of the ultimate recourse—war."* This essay was first published in the January 1972 issue of* The Freeman *and later became a chapter in Dr. Carson's book,* The Rebirth of Liberty: The Founding of the American Republic, 1760–1800 *(first published by Arlington House in 1973 and later by FEE in 1976).*

What provoked the American colonists to resist British acts, to rebel against restrictions placed upon them, and eventually to declare and effect their independence? To put the matter in more conventional terms: What caused the American Revolution?

Men who have spent years studying the questions propound different answers. Some hold that the British mercantile system provided the provocation to revolt. Others have held that the American colonists benefited from mercantilism and that, this being so, mercantilism was hardly at the root of the difficulty. Another thesis that has been argued, most persuasively by Lawrence Henry Gipson, is that the American colonies had attained a level of maturity that made them no longer dependent upon Britain and no longer desirous of the connection. Some historians have gone so far as to charge that American debtors with the desire to rid themselves of pressing British creditors stirred up resistance and brought off a revolution. Those looking for a class struggle explanation of the confict have tried to make the revolt against Britain a part of an internal struggle between the haves and have-nots. In short, almost every interpretation that could be imagined has been offered, and many of these have been buttressed by impressive arguments and such evidence as fitted them.

One thing is about as clear as such things can ever be: mercantilist acts did not provoke the initial resistance in the mid-1760's. The Stamp Act of 1765 was not a mercantilist act, nor was the Sugar Act of 1764 primarily mercantilistic. Indeed, the Sugar Act altered some of the original mercantilist features of the Molasses Act of an earlier date. Moreover, there had been mercantilist restrictions on the American colonists for more than a century, and none of these had provoked violent resistance. There can be no doubt that colonists were long since used to mercantilist restrictions, and peoples are unlikely to revolt against that to which they have become accustomed. The fact is that when representatives of the colonists gathered at the Stamp Act Congress to air their grievances, they announced that what they fundamentally opposed was "taxation without representation," a thing contrary to the British constitution. They readily granted—at first—that Britain had the right to regulate their commerce. It follows, then, that the immediate provocation to resistance was not mercantilist measures.

But this is only to look at things from the surface and to wrench them out of a much broader historical context where they belong. Suppose that instead of asking why and what the colonists resisted we ask why the British persisted in passing measures which provoked the colonists. More directly, why did Parliament attempt to raise revenues from the colonies in ways that departed from custom and long established policy? Why did they lay direct and indirect taxes on the colonies?

For Revenue Only

The answers to these questions are not far to seek. The British government was in dire need of new sources of revenue. The wars of the eighteenth century had been highly expensive, and the indebtedness of the government was mounting. The debt in 1755—just prior to the Seven Year's War (or French and Indian War as it was known in America)—stood at about £75,000,000. By 1766 it had mounted to £133,000,000.[1] The British people were heavily taxed, and new taxes were being added. The reaction in the mother country to an added tax on domestic cider is instructive. "The news of the passing of the cider act was the signal for 'tumults and riots' in the apple-growing counties of England, and many producers of cider threatened to cut down their orchards if the excise were collected.''[2] In short, the heavily taxed British were in no mood to accept additional burdens.

By contrast, American colonists were generally lightly taxed, and several colonies had no government debt to speak of. For example, one historian describes the situation in Pennsylvania in this way: "Not only were the inhabitants relieved of all *ordinary* charges of government during the years 1760–63 but, aside from a revived excise tax on liquors, they also enjoyed such relief during the remainder of the period down to the Revolution. Moreover, the personal and estate taxes . . . represented a per capita levy of less than one shilling . . ." by 1775.[3] A report from Maryland in 1767 indicated that "all levies for the support of the provincial government—in contrast to those for the support of the clergy, the schools, and other county and parish charges— amounted to less than £5,500, an annual per capita tax of about a shilling."[4] Though not all the colonies had such a pleasant tax situation, neither was it generally unpleasant. On top of this, colonial governments had been reimbursed for their military outlays during the French and Indian War.

If these conditions be accepted at face value, if there be no looking behind them, it would appear that the case of Britain's taxing the colonists would certainly be understandable and probably justifiable. But the situation does warrant an examination of the background. British taxation of the colonists broke a long-term contract with them—so the colonists said—and heralded a major policy turn. Back of this policy shift were the mercantilistic policies and practices which had produced a domestic crisis for the British which their government tried to relieve by bringing pressure on the colonies.

Bitter Fruits of History

The contradictions of mercantilism had produced a long harvest of bitter fruit, some of which the British government and people were no longer willing to accept. No more, in justice, could the American colonists be expected to accept them. It is true that the debates of the 1760s and 1770s were not usually conducted in terms of mercantile policy. The contradictions were there, however, and policy changes should be viewed in the light of them. During this time, Adam Smith was putting together his monumental work, *The Wealth of Nations*, which laid bare the fallacies and contradictions of mercantilism. It may be accounted appropriate, too, that this work appeared in print in 1776, the same year as the Declaration of Independence. A little examination into British mercantilism will show its role in producing an impasse between Britain and America.

Mercantilism was a composite of ideas and practices which had grown helter-skelter over a couple of centuries before the revolt in the American colonies. Most of the ideas were formulated in the seventeenth and eighteenth centuries, but some of the practices associated with it are much older. The theory of mercantilism was the first faltering effort at devising a general theory of economics in the modern era. As some thinkers cut loose from a Christian framework and attempted to look at things naturally, they devised a crude economics to fit new preconceptions. The theory was weighted down with two assumptions, however, which were cultural in origin rather than natural.

Measured in Gold

The first of these assumptions was made up largely of what is commonly called the bullion theory. Bullionism is the notion that wealth consists of precious metals, particularly gold, and that the value of everything else derives from the fact that precious metals will be exchanged for it. It is understandable that men should have come to think in this way. Gold was the most universally acceptable medium of exchange in both East and West. It hardly deteriorates; it weighs little in proportion to its exchange value for other things; it has many practical uses; and it is malleable. Men ever and again mistake money, because it can be exchanged for goods, for the source of the value which their demand gives the goods. Small wonder, then, they should make this confusion about gold when gold is valued as a commodity as well as a medium of exchange.

The second major assumption of mercantilism was nationalistic. That is, mercantilists thought exclusively about how a single nation might enhance its wealth by increasing its supply of gold. One nation's wealth, as they saw it, was usually gained at the expense of another nation. Ordinarily, one nation gains gold from another nation which is losing its supply. (It is interesting to speculate that mercantilistic theory and practice may well have been born out of the intense desire of many countries to separate the Spanish from the great hordes of gold they had found in the Americas.) According to the bullion theory, then, one nation's wealth is increased by diminishing that of another.

The thrust of mercantilism was to make trade into a contest among the governments of nations. This was so because trade was now conceived of as a potential means for increasing the bullion holdings of a nation. This would be accomplished, according to mercantilists, by way of a favorable balance of trade. A favorable balance of trade is said to exist when the goods and services which one nation sells to another exceeds those bought from the other. In brief, a nation had a favorable balance of trade when exports exceeded imports. This was thought to be "favorable" because the difference would be made up in gold and the "wealth" of the nation thus favored would be augmented. A nation which imported more than it exported would, of course, have an unfavorable balance of trade.

Numerous practices which might help a nation to get a favorable balance of trade were contrived or justified by this theory. The practices were usually aimed at increasing exports and decreasing imports. Imports could be decreased if more of the goods consumed in a country were produced there. To that end governments encouraged manufacturing by special charters and encouraged the growing of certain crops by subsidies and bounties. Of course, imports were more directly discouraged by tariffs, quotas, and discriminatory charges levied against foreign suppliers. Similar practices also might help a country to increase its exports.

Colonies were conceived of as being particularly valuable in enhancing the wealth of a nation. Frequently wanted were raw materials for manufacturing as well as produce which could not be grown economically at home. If such exotic products could be acquired from colonies they need not be imported from some other country. In addition to this, a colony might have an unfavorable balance of trade with the mother country and thus be a source of the precious metals it would send to make up the trade deficit.

The American continental colonies were part of a British empire which had been shaped in the seventeenth and eighteenth centuries as a result of the mercantile policies of England. Initially, the kings of England had attempted to plant and benefit from colonies by granting them as monopolies to private companies and proprietors. These companies and individuals were empowered to regulate the activities of those who came over so that the undertakings would benefit the owners and, perchance, enhance the wealth and power of England. Things did not work out that way very consistently. Colonists frequently cared little enough about whether they benefited the original charter holders or not; instead, they concentrated their efforts on doing what was to their own benefit. Moreover, as colonists gained some measure of control over their governments, they often enacted their own mercantile policies with the intent of making a colony self-sufficient.[5] Such action ran counter to British aims, of course.

Acts of Intervention

By the mid-seventeenth century, then, Britain was ready to begin to impose a general system of mercantile restrictions on the colonists.

The most general of the mercantile acts are those known as the Navigation Acts. A series of these acts was passed over the years from 1651 through 1663. The number of acts passed was increased because legislation passed in the 1650's was considered invalid after the restoration of monarchy in 1660. This being the case, the later acts are the only ones that need concern us here. The Navigation Act of 1660—reenacted in 1661—required that all trade with the colonies be carried in English-built ships which were manned predominantly by Englishmen. "English" was defined for this purpose to include the inhabitants of the colonies. All foreign merchants were excluded from the commerce of the English colonies, and certain enumerated articles, e.g., tobacco, could be exported from the colonies only to Britain or British possessions. The Staple Act of 1663 provided that goods to be exported from European countries to English colonies must first be shipped to England.

"These acts intended to give England a monopoly of the trade of her colonies," one historian notes:

> —not a monopoly to particular persons, but a national monopoly in which all English merchants should share. The Staple Act meant not only that English merchants would get the business of selling to the colonies but also that English manufacturers might dispose of their wares at an advantage in that the foreign goods which had to pass through England en route to the colonies might be taxed, thereby raising their prices and enabling English goods to undersell them. Similarly, the enumerated article principle assured that most of the colonial staples important to England would be exported by English merchants, who were also guaranteed employment for their vessels through the exclusion of foreign vessels from the English colonies.[6]

Parliament passed another Navigation Act in 1696, but it was only an effort to tighten the administration of existing law rather than to add new features.[7]

British legislation also attempted to prevent certain kinds of manufacturing and trade from developing in the colonies. The Woolens Act of 1699 prohibited the export of wool or woolen goods from a colony either to other colonies or to other countries. The Hat Act of 1732 prohibited the exportation of hats from the colony in which they were made, and limited the number of apprentices a hatmaker might have. The Molasses Act of 1733 placed high duties on molasses, sugar, and rum imported into the colonies from any source other than British colonies. This was an attempt to give the British West Indies a virtual monopoly of the trade. It may also have been intended to increase income from the tariff or to reduce the shipping activities of New Englanders. The Iron Act of 1750 permitted pig iron to be exported from the colonies to England duty free but prohibited the erection of new iron mills for the finishing of products in the colonies.

There were other types of mercantile regulations than those above. Over the years, it was usually illegal for specie (gold coins) to be exported from England to the colonies. The British tried to encourage production of wanted goods in the colonies by paying bounties. For example, the British government paid these premiums to importers of colonial naval stores: "£4 a ton for pitch and tar; £3 a ton for resin and turpentine; £6 a ton for hemp; and £1 a ton for masts, yards, and bowsprits."[8]

The purpose of all these regulations and restrictions was to make the colonies profitable to Britain, of course. To that end, the colonists were encouraged to produce goods which could not be competitively produced in England, discouraged to compete with the mother country, encouraged to send specie to England, discouraged from receiving specie from that country, and discouraged from developing markets in America which could serve either England or other countries. There were, however, many unwanted side effects of these policies. They are commonly referred to as the inner contradictions of mercantilism.

The Road to War

The most dire result of mercantilism was war. Indeed, some believe that mercantilism did not so much lead to war as war led to mercantilism. One writer says that the "needs of constant warfare, especially its costs, had encouraged every power to develop and marshal its resources, attempting to become self-sufficient, especially in the sinews of war. . . . This economic nationalism, generally described as *mercantilism*, is less a theory than a weapon—the use of economic means to serve political ends."[9] There is no doubt that mercantilist methods were used sometimes in warfare, but the usual causal relation is the other way around. Mercantilism ranges government power behind the commercial activities of a nation, uses government power to support the merchants of a nation against those of other nations, prohibits trade activities of foreigners in order to give advantages to native tradesmen. In order to support or protect their tradesmen, other nations retaliated with similar restrictions and sought colonies which would be protected trade areas for their people. If trade is free, competition is peaceful, but mercantilism shifts the contest into the realm of governmental power. When governments contest for advantage in this way they are moving in the direction of the ultimate recourse—war.

Such were the results of mercantilism in the seventeenth and eighteenth centuries. War followed upon war with monotonous regularity as naval and colonial powers contested with one another for dominance and advantages. The wars between the British and Dutch in the mid-seventeenth century were clearly mercantile in origin and character. Nettels notes that the Navigation Act of 1651 "precipitated the First Anglo-Dutch War of 1652–54."[10] Further, he says that the "acts of 1660–63 threatened to exclude the Dutch completely from the English colonies and consequently new fuel was added to the old rivalry. In 1664 occurred the Second Anglo-Dutch War. . . . "[11] It was not simply incidental, either, that during this conflict the English gained control of the Middle Colonies in America. A third war broke out in 1672. "Although a Dutch fleet recaptured New Amsterdam in August 1673 the treaty of peace in 1674 once more restored it to England—an act which marked the passing of the Dutch menace to England's North American trade."[12]

Unfortunately, it did not end the rivalry in North America nor the train of mercantilistic wars. France was now emerging in the latter part of the seventeenth century as a major power under the aggressive leadership of Louis XIV. Louis courted English monarchs so that they would allow him room to operate to fulfill his ambitions on the continent of Europe. The courtship may have been the undoing of Charles II and James II; at any rate, it came to an end with the Glorious Revolution in 1688. A Dutchman, William of Orange, became William III of England and joint ruler with his wife Mary during the rest of her lifetime. In very short order, Britain went to war with France (King William's War) and by so doing began a series of conflicts with that nation which did not finally end until the Congress of Vienna in 1815. Since other nations and their possessions were usually involved in these conflicts between England and France, these wars may well be called world wars.

While King William's War of the 1690's was ostensibly fought to maintain a balance of power in Europe, the colonies were at stake, also, at least potentially. One history indicates that in issuing his declaration of war "William took cognizance of the offenses of Louis' subjects in America against the English colonies there—in Newfoundland, in Hudson Bay, in the West Indies, in New York, and in Nova Scotia."[13] Though there was considerable fighting in America, there were no significant territorial changes as a result of that war.

Maps of North America showing territorial possessions of European powers and changes in them from 1700–1763 indicate something of the bearing of the colonial situation on the great wars of this period. In 1700, the English held only a relatively narrow strip of the eastern coast of North America from New England to Georgia, with claims running back to the Appalachian mountain chain generally. Most of the territory which is now Canada was then claimed by France, along with the vast hinterland region drained by the Mississippi River. South and west of these were the extensive Spanish possessions. The English hold on the continent was still precarious, and the colonies were surrounded except on the side of the Atlantic Ocean by territory claimed by other European powers. This situation would be dramatically altered by 1763 as a result of the wars.

A Struggle for Control

The War of the Spanish Succession (1702–13, known in England as Queen Anne's War) was fought over issues which were tied to the question of who would dominate the Americas. Louis XIV was determined that his grandson should become king of Spain immediately and should eventually succeed him to the throne of France. This would not only bring under one person two great powers in Europe but would also link two massive empires in America. This was an intolerable prospect for England. As one history puts the matter: "For Holland and England, it was a war over colonies and trade. These two countries were determined to prevent a union of the French and Spanish crowns; but they were above all determined to prevent France from getting into a position to block their own commercial and territorial ambitions in America.''[14] At the conclusion of the war, provisions were made for perpetual separation of the French and Spanish crowns, and Britain gained new territory in America: Newfoundland, Acadia, and the Hudson Bay territory.

England got involved in war with Spain in 1739, known as the War of Jenkin's Ear, and a part of the struggle was over possession of Georgia. There was some fighting in America, but it was very limited, for the conflict shifted to Europe and the more general convulsion known as the War of the Austrian Succession (1740–48). This war did not result in any territorial changes, though there were changes in alliances on the continent of Europe which affected future events.

The peace that followed this second of world wars in the eighteenth century was unusually brief. The French and Indian War broke out in America, 1754; it involved most basically a contest over territory in what is now western Pennsylvania between the French and Indians on the one hand and the British and English Americans on the other. As an extension of this conflict, a general war broke out in Europe in 1756, known as the Seven Year's War. A major conflict continued in America, reaching its climax with the Battle of Quebec in 1759. There the British forces decisively defeated the French. By the Treaty of Paris of 1763, the British got all the French Canadian holdings and French and Spanish territory east of the Mississippi.

The British had apparently emerged triumphant in these wars against France. The American colonies now had an extensive domain to be opened up and exploited; it was a long way to the frontiers of any other European colonial power. A vast British empire had been acquired and was ready for the shaping.

So it may have looked to an imperialist, but the British Parliament and people were confronted with grave difficulties in the wake of the apparent triumph. There was, as earlier told, a huge debt in England in 1763 as a result of the wars. It was a debt of a size that would most likely dwarf all the profits gained thus far from mercantilist policies. But even if the balance books had stood otherwise, the contradictions of mercantilism would still, most likely, have produced an impasse.

One of the fallacies of mercantilism is that the wealth within a nation constitutes the wealth of a nation. Wealth in Britain was not distributed among the inhabitants equally but individually possessed. Undoubtedly, some merchants, manufacturers, shippers, and tradesmen extracted great wealth as a result of special favors within the mercantile system. But this need not have increased the wealth of the populace in general. Indeed, when it is understood that mercantile policies restricted the entry of goods from other lands and raised their prices, it becomes clear that the populace in general frequently suffered rather than benefited from mercantilism. When the burden of taxes to pay for mercantile wars was added to this—taxes levied on the populace in general—it is easy to understand why there was widespread dissatisfaction in Britain.

Of course, the British government did not proclaim mercantilism a failure. Even if this had been clearly understood at the time, it is doubtful that those in power would have reversed their policies. At any rate, they did not do so. Instead, they laid the blame for difficulties on American evasion of mercantile restrictions, determined to enforce them more vigorously, and declared that the Americans must be taxed to help pay for the wars, a portion of which had been fought in their defense.

This course of action seemed eminently fair to many Englishmen. After all, the colonists had been prime beneficiaries of British protection. Moreover, many Americans were reported to be living well if not luxuriously. Not only that, but to make matters worse, these colonists paid very little by way of taxes. Such expenses as they had incurred in the recent French and Indian War had been reimbursed from the British treasury. Surely, there could be no reasonable objection to mild taxation of the colonists. As a matter of fact, there could and would be, but we have not yet come to that part of the story.

Victims or Beneficiaries?

What is most relevant here is the impact of mercantilism on the American colonies. The question has been raised by some historians as to whether the colonists were not really the beneficiaries of British mercantilism rather than the victims. The fact that many Americans prospered under the system is submitted as evidence that they benefited from the system. There is also negative evidence that Americans had rough going economically after the break from England. The reasoning underlying this argument confuses *becauses of* with *in spite of*. The thrust of mercantilism is not such that it would produce prosperity in general for those on whom it is imposed. Its thrust is to siphon resources from the colonies (and other countries) into the mother country. To restrict manufacturing, to deny the development of local markets, to constrict intercolonial trade, and to make the mother country the port of entry for many goods could hardly benefit the colonists generally.

Perhaps the most fundamental flaw of mercantilism is the view that a nation's wealth can be increased by exporting more in goods and services than is imported. This policy was quite harmful to colonies without providing corresponding benefits to Britain. The British succeeded in a "favorable" balance of trade with the American mainland colonies. The most immediate effect was the gold drain from the colonies to Britain. This tendency was augmented by prohibiting the export of gold from Britain. Moreover, many of the ways by which the colonists might have made up the difference were denied to them by mercantile restrictions.

In consequence, the colonists suffered a shortage of specie. The practical effect was that colonists paid higher prices for goods coming from England than they would have had to do if a free market in gold had existed, because gold was more plentiful in Britain than in America. It is even doubtful that British merchants benefited from this situation as much as might be supposed, for they usually made loans to Americans to enable them to buy their goods. Americans also had their credit in England augmented by such payments as reimbursement for participation in wars (an augmentation at the expense of British taxpayers).

Much of the economic activity within the colonies was an uphill effort to overcome the ill effects of mercantile policies. Probably, the fixing of slavery so extensively can be ascribed in the main to mercantilism. (British policy was opposed to the emancipation of slaves because slaves were frequently collateral for loans.) Planters were driven to expand their production—to the acquisition of more and more slaves—in the often vain hope of balancing their trade. The Triangular Trade by New Englanders, which included the slave trade, was an extended effort to get specie. The paper money emissions which became so common toward the close of the period were efforts to deal with the monetary crisis. Of course, many of the efforts of colonists to find ways to deal with the situation were prohibited before they were well established.

1. Lawrence H. Gipson, *The Coming of the Revolution* (New York: Harper Torchbooks, 1962), pp. 55–56.

2. *Ibid.*, p. 58.

3. *Ibid.*, p. 136.

4. *Ibid.*, p. 138.

5. See E. A. J. Johnson, *American Economic Thought in the Seventeenth Century* (New York: Russell and Russell, 1961), pp. 8–29.

6. Curtis P. Nettels, *The Roots of American Civilization* (New York: Appleton-Century-Crofts, 1963, 2nd ed.), p. 283.

7. *Ibid.*, p. 375.

8. *Ibid.*, p. 434.

9. Eugen Weber, *A Modern History of Europe* (New York: Norton, 1971), pp. 145–46.

10. Nettels, *op. cit.*, p. 281.

11. *Ibid.*, p. 283.

12. *Ibid.*, p. 284.

13. Max Sevelle and Robert Middlekauff, *A History of Colonial America* (New York: Holt, Rinehart and Winston, 1964, rev. ed.), p. 261.

14. *Ibid.*, p. 265.

6

Native Pottery Only

by William L. Baker

The American Civil War also had its ironies connected with protectionism. William L. Baker, a teacher in the school system in Lubbock, Texas, uses a seldom remarked-on paradox of the Civil War to make an economic point in this article that first appeared in The Freeman *in December, 1978. At the time that the Union was successfully blockading the ports of the South in a military move that ultimately led to victory for the blockading forces, Congress was impeding the Union economy with protective tariffs, on the premise that foreign goods destroy domestic business. If this were true, Baker asks, why didn't the North call off its blockade and let the forces of free trade destroy the South?*

T he Civil War had just begun. The nation's new President, Abraham Lincoln, had received the news of the bombardment of Fort Sumter with a great deal of trepidation. Now it was his turn to act. But what to do? How best to meet this challenge to the armed might of the United States of America? Shortly after the news of Fort Sumter reached Lincoln, he had closeted himself in conference with the venerable hero and Chief of Staff, General Winfield Scott. As usual, Scott had some answers.

One of Scott's solutions particularly struck home with the new President. During the course of their meeting, General Scott had repeatedly emphasized the necessity of forming a naval blockade of all the Southern ports in order to isolate the fledgling Confederacy and cut off their foreign trade. And, while this would be an expensive maneuver involving hundreds of ships and thousands of men, it would be essential in weakening and curbing as quickly as possible the armies of the rebellion.

The reasoning behind this was very simple: besides being the oldest tactic in military history—tried, tested, and proven—it stood to reason that the fewer imports a nation (or city) receives from outside sources the worse off it becomes economically and, thus, militarily. Military experts had always realized that trade and commerce were the lifeblood of a nation and that the sooner it could be stopped the better it was for the opposing side. Such a blockade, Scott realized, would spell doom to the enemy.

So on April 19, 1861, Abraham Lincoln, along with General Winfield Scott, devised the blockade that would be put into effect as soon as possible. This plan, which later became known as the "anaconda plan," was to prove instrumental in crushing the life out of the vibrant Southern economy. In no time at all Admiral Porter of the Union navy had put the paper plan into effect. He would make the South writhe and groan until they would eventually have to sue for peace. In later years the Supreme Court declared the "anaconda plan" as the official beginning of the War Between the States.

As the Union ships were engaged in the vital task of squeezing the enemy dry, what were the President and the Congress doing back home? Why nothing other than devising elaborate and prohibitive tariff schedules in order to keep the "invasion" of "foreign" products out of the Union! Imports would surely destroy the Northern cause, they reasoned. What the North needed most of all was "protection." So while Union ships blockaded the South by sea, the honorable Congress was doing the same thing to the North at home. What Southern sea captains could never once accomplish in four years of war, the Congress did for them in a matter of weeks by political action.

The Blockade of the North

Barriers to trade rose higher than ever before in the attempt to "protect" the North. Confederate ships were therefore freed to prowl the lanes further out on the high seas since the boys in Washington were doing such an admirable job without them. They could now have more leisure to ferret out those few merchantmen who were officially allowed through the lines. They could also find more of those who simply chose to bear the risks of smuggling goods into Yankee ports and hamlets. In this respect Confederate vessels actually found themselves as enforcers of the Congressional mandate of restricted trade! Confederate raiders made no distinction between "legal" or "illegal" trade.

What is often neglected in the history of the Civil War is not the "blockade runners" of the South who have received plenty of plaudits for their daring exploits, but the "blockade runners" of the North who had their work cut out for them by attempting to slip the blockade of the Northern coast by Northern ships and customs agents that their own Congress had imposed upon the country at the very beginning of the war.

Apparently the logic of the situation never once dawned upon the President or the Congress that acted so hastily to put his economic plans into effect. If the North was "protecting" Union industry from the evil effects of international trade by Congressional action, wasn't it doing the same by anchoring warships off Southern ports for better than three thousand miles? The story of Haman, who unknowingly built his own gallows, could not have been more ironic!

And when the tariff blockade seemed to be developing leaks, Congress merely tightened the garrote a bit tighter around the North's windpipe, thus choking off needed manpower and supplies which Europe had to offer. All the while this little tragi-comic charade was going on, there were actually Union leaders who felt that more warships were needed to blockade the South in order to catch the blockade runners who were slipping through the net.

What the Congress should have done in order to be consistent with their own untenable economic doctrines would have been to recall every Union ship, scrap the blockade, and let the South kill itself from the "invasion" of "foreign" goods which would surely "glut" the domestic market, thus "flooding" the Southern economy with products which would destroy business and bring the war to a hasty conclusion!

Fortunately for the North, the Union navy was more efficient in destroying the Southern trade than the Congress was in choking off Union supplies. But try as they might, the politicians in the capital could not outshine the navy on the high seas. It is true that the solons inflicted incalculable damage upon the Northern market during the course of the war. But the few Northern ships that were assigned to blockade the Northern coast simply could not inflict the kind of damage to Union-bound shipping that their more numerous colleagues assigned to block the Southern coast could inflict upon the South. As a result, the North floundered along without the full benefits of trade with a Europe that was more than willing to provide the materials so desperately needed to terminate the war.

Continuing War on Trade

Most historians dwell at great length upon the comparative advantages of the North over the South during the Civil War. That which usually receives the greatest emphasis is the higher productivity and resources of the North. And while all this is true, it fails to consider the resources and productivity *that could have been available* had free trade been allowed. In effect it is not so much the pounding that the South gave the North during the war, but rather the pounding which Congress gave the North, by depriving itself of the benefits of free trade, that deserves more attention.

Today warships continue to prowl the coastlines and to ply the lanes of commerce in order to "shield" the nation from the "invasion" of Australian beef, Japanese steel, and so forth. Even in this modern age the old trade-is-war doctrine contines to guide national policy. The United States continues to look at "foreign" goods as a calamity to be avoided at all costs. Recent broadsides against the market prove that the spirit of tyranny and war still lives in the hearts and the minds of the "planners" and policymakers. These bombasts seem to come ever closer to the waterline of the market and its functions. Yet, in spite of it all, the market continues to operate—if at a much reduced level of efficiency.

This attempt to bring the economics of warfare to the market has resulted in untold misery for all of mankind who stand to benefit from the cosmopolitanism of the free market. This perpetual assault on trade and the well-being it brings has offered, instead of a vast cornucopia of wealth, the specter of the pale horse and the pale rider of war and man-made famine. The doctrine of "protectionism" has never resulted in anything other than planned chaos. Nor is this a doctrine that has sprung up full grown from the ashes and motivations of the War Between the States. As far back as the days of the Greek Herodotus in the fifth century B.C. we are told that it was against the law for anything that was of Athenian origin to be brought into a certain Greek temple. Only "native" pottery would do. "Protectionists" were alive and well in his day too.

It is no different in our day. We still hear arguments about the "evils" of "foreign" products, arguments which were exploded by economists generations ago. We still hear preached as official ideology the tragedies and horrors of allowing the market to "flood" us with a "glut" of "cheap" goods which the international (foreign) market has to offer. We see farmers blocking roads on the Mexican border, attacking trucks as policemen stand by and sympathetically witness the carnage. We see organizations of such men who call themselves "soldiers" (in the true spirit of warfare) pleading for "sympathy and under-standing" from their fellow citizens. We hear the neat little cliches that are intended to take the place of ideas and intelligent thought. We hear the martial strains of propaganda telling us to "rally round the flag." After all it *is* "Our America."

The tones and pleas of the petty provincialists of trade restriction have not changed one bit over the eleven decades since the Civil War. Neither have the effects of their policies which continue to be a blight upon men and an assault on intelligence wherever and whenever such doctrines are implemented. The war on the market—and thus civilization—goes on.

Native pottery only, please!

7

Agricultural Technology, Economic Incentives, and World Food Problems

by E. C. Pasour, Jr.

People must eat, whatever else they do without. Surely, say the protectionists, we must therefore support and maintain our farmers, and we will also produce enough to feed the starving abroad. In this essay that first appeared in the July 1985 Freeman, *E. C. Pasour, Jr., Professor of Economics at North Carolina State University in Raleigh, finds this attitude tragically mistaken. Dramatic technological breakthroughs have increased agricultural productivity in both developed and developing countries to the point where there is no doubt that free trade could release the food to feed the world and wipe out famine. Not only do collectivist policies in underdeveloped countries perpetuate famine there, but the support of farmers by government programs in developed countries, like the United States, is actually contributing to a situation that makes things worse for the hungry in less developed nations.*

B ritish Parson Sir Thomas Malthus predicted in 1798 that population increases over time would outstrip increases in food production causing chronic food shortages. In recent years, a neo-Malthusian doctrine has again gained popularity as widespread hunger problems, especially in Ethiopia and other African countries, command front-page headlines. It is ironic that visions of a starving Africa are obscuring a major surge in agricultural productivity throughout much of the world today. Moreover, there is a great deal of evidence that the most serious constraints on food production are not weather or natural resources but rather government policies that stifle entrepreneurial incentives. This paper presents evidence on rising farm productivity, the importance of economic incentives in agriculture, and implications for world food production and economic development.

Rising Farm Productivity

Increases in agricultural technology are resulting in dramatic increases in farm productivity throughout much of the world.[1] In the United States, farmers planted the world's first hybrid wheat in 1984, which increased yields from 25 to 30 per cent. Rice growers in the Gulf states planted a new rice variety, which also had yields 25 to 30 per cent higher than earlier varieties. At the same time, Taiwanese farmers are feeding surplus rice to livestock. Agricultural output is also increasing rapidly in the European Economic Community (E.E.C.). Wheat yields rose 23 per cent in the E.E.C. in 1984 and French harvest of field peas has jumped 50 per cent in two years.

Contrary to popular impression, world agricultural production is also increasing rapidly in the developing countries. Thailand, Malaysia, Indonesia, and the Philippines have all increased their farm productivity by more than 35 per cent in the last decade. The International Rice Research Institute has introduced its Third World rice variety, which requires much less nitrogen and pesticide protection to achieve yields comparable to those of its previous "miracle" rice varieties. Researchers in Peru are making break-throughs in production in the huge Amazon Basin replacing trace minerals that leach rapidly because of the high rainfall. Argentine wheat has become so cheap that grain companies recently considered importing it into the United States.

Agricultural productivity in Asia has been most influenced by the Green Revolution and by a recent dramatic shift in Chinese farm policy. Green Revolution rice varieties have been the biggest single factor in lifting Asian agricultural output by more than 25 per cent during the past decade. Yet, potential gains from increases in available technology can be choked by policies that stifle entrepreneurial incentives.

Technology Is Not Enough

China provides a classic example both of the effect of collectivist agricultural policies and of what can happen when these policies are changed. In 1958, Chairman Mao decreed "The Year of the Great Leap Forward." Under the "Great Leap Program," large numbers of farm workers were to be diverted to industrial employment and the remaining farm population forced into agricultural communes. The loss in agricultural output caused by these policies was catastrophic. Food supplies fell to famine levels and had not recovered by 1965. Thus, contrary to conventional wisdom, per capita food consumption actually decreased during the Mao years.

China's agricultural output has increased dramatically since the late 1970s when a decision was made to increase farm product prices, scrap the big communal farms, and lease the land back to families and small groups. The privatization moves and the retreat from communism have been accompanied by an increase in food grain output of 12 per cent a year for the past seven years despite bad weather in 1980, so that China has overtaken Russia as the world's largest wheat producer.[2]

A recent article in *The Economist* reveals a general relationship between market incentives and agricultural production.[3] In a cross-country comparison of food production, Africa dominates the list of individual countries whose agriculture has increased the least since 1970. However, the difference between the most and least productive African states is dramatic. Significantly, the study concludes that: "Those which have done best—e.g., Ivory Coast and Malawi—have encouraged private ownership of land, or given peasant farmers security of tenure. The least productive have been those which have encouraged state and collective farms."[4]

The evidence suggests that property rights and economic incentives are fully as important in less developed as in highly developed economies. This conclusion, however, should not be taken to mean that providing economic incentives will quickly transform a poor country. There is no short-cut to economic development, with or without outside financial aid. (As shown below, financial aid often is counterproductive.)

The solution to economic development in low-income countries lies primarily within the countries themselves. The only long-run solution to food and income problems in any country is to increase through capital formation the productivity of the people involved. When government policies severely distort economic incentives and discourage capital formation, it is not surprising that productivity, including agricultural output, is low.

What Can Be Done?

There is evidence that more can be done to increase food production in poor countries. Large increases in output by peasants in India, China, and other countries show that increases in agricultural output do not require big farms, big dams, big irrigation systems or an "agricultural plan." Instead, the most important step is to provide entrepreneurial incentives. This means that poor countries needs to scrap those policies that are biased against farmers such as high taxes, price controls on farm products, overvalued exchange rates that depress agricultural exports, and protectionist trade policies that increase the cost of fertilizer and farm machinery.[5]

Developing countries, for example, often have regulations banning the importation of tractors, harvesters, and other mechanically powered farm machinery. Such restrictions are based on the old but persistent myth that machines destroy jobs. This argument carried to its logical conclusion would prevent all substitution of capital for labor and permanently keep workers at a subsistence level.

Another important step, as suggested by the productivity figures presented above, is to increase the application of science in agricultural production. Per capita food production rose 16 per cent in South America and 10 per cent in Asia between 1972 and 1982.[6] This improved performance is due both to improved farming technology and to stronger economic incentives to use it. Many small farmers in developing countries, given an incentive, can now benefit from higher yielding varieties and better pest control.

Africa—No Exception

But what about Africa? In recent months, the world's attention has been riveted on Africa's hunger problems. The food problem in Africa is not due to the lack of natural resources. The problem is that most of Africa has continued to practice its traditional method of cultivation as rising population pressures allow fallow land less and less time to recover its natural fertility. Overgrazing is also encouraged by communal landholding. Public policies rooted in a development model stressing the necessity of central planning and rapid industrialization stifle agricultural production (and economic development in general). Dennis Avery, senior agricultural analyst, U.S. Department of State, presents a vivid example:

> The importance of policy is amply demonstrated in the neighboring countries of Kenya and Tanzania. The two nations have similar agricultural resources and histories—but in the 20 years since independence, they have followed diametrically opposite farm policies. Kenya divided big land-holdings among smallholders, then backed the smallholders with price incentives, research and extension programs. Overall farm productivity increased 37 per cent from 1971 to 1982. Tanzania forced its scattered family farmers to consolidate into large villages . . . Tanzania's farm output rose only 12 per cent in the 11 years from 1971 to 1982—even by the Tanzanian government's highly optimistic numbers. Only massive food aid forestalled widespread hunger in Tanzania even before the recent drought.[7]

Avery contends that even in Africa, technology is now available to double yields and drought-proof its food supplies.[8] He cites as evidence a new, more drought-resistant sorghum hybrid developed in the Sudan that appears to have the potential to triple yields in much of East Africa. Also available is a new sorghum for the dryer region of the Sahel that apparently can double yields there. In West Africa, there is the potential to become self-sufficient in rice by shifting from upland to swamp rice production. Nigeria has a new corn variety that yielded nine tons per hectare in the midst of last year's drought (the current average yield is one ton). New peanut varieties with yields several times those of current varieties are being tested in Senegal, Mozambique, Zambia, and Zimbabwe. Improved pest control and new varieties helped bring about a seven-fold increase in yields of cowpeas in West Africa. The fact that available technology has not been more widely applied in Africa is not only a highly visible human tragedy but also an indictment of the government policies of African nations.

Farm Programs in Developed Countries

Agricultural success in the less developed countries is also adversely affected by farm programs in the United States and other highly developed countries that subsidize domestic agricultural output. When domestic prices of farm products are raised above the world price, imports must be restricted to prevent domestic users from buying lower priced imports. As a result of the U.S. sugar price support program, for example, domestic sugar price was four times the world price in late 1984. This import quota system, imposed by the world's biggest sugar market, is highly detrimental to Caribbean sugar producers.

In addition, subsidies, easy credit terms, and reduced interest rates are often used in the United States, the European Economic Community, and other developed countries to increase agricultural exports. Regardless of the type subsidy, producers in the exporting country receive an artificial advantage at the expense of producers in the countries where the products are "dumped." This dumping of agricultural products in developing countries permits governments to keep the price of food cheap to the detriment of local farmers. Dependence on cheap imports discourages agricultural development and food production. The conclusion is that in assisting developing countries, the United States, the E.E.C., and other highly developed countries should stop subsidizing their own farmers. While government farm programs in the United States are often sold to the public on the basis of helping "feed the world," these programs actually impede economic development and food production in less-developed countries.

Economic Aid

The conventional wisdom for the past generation has been that poor countries cannot develop without financial aid from the highly developed countries. Foreign aid, however, is not indispensable to economic progress. Indeed, P.T. Bauer shows that aid is more likely to obstruct development than to promote it.[9] Foreign aid reduces incomes in the donor countries and enables the recipient country to follow counterproductive interventionist policies. Aid, for example, enabled Tanzania to pursue economic and social policies that are antithetical to both economic progress and individual freedom. The effects on farm output of the Tanzanian experiment (which involved forcibly herding millions of people into collectivized villages) were described above.

Neo-Malthusians frequently cite the population "explosion" as an insurmountable barrier in alleviating world hunger. The prophets of doom typically reach their conclusions on the basis of projecting past trends. However, there is no reason to expect population to continue to increase at the same rate in developing countries as economic development occurs. When income levels rise in developing countries, the birth rate can be expected to decrease.[10] Thus, the relationship between population and food must be considered in the context of economic development. There is no evidence that Draconian population controls (such as compulsory sterilization or abortion) are required for economic development.

Implications and Conclusions

The world is currently undergoing a major increase in agricultural productivity. World agricultural production is at a record high and is increasing rapidly. Agricultural output is increasing rapidly in the developing countries—rising from 2.7 per cent per year in the early 1970s to 3.3 per cent annually from 1977 to 1982.[11] This growth rate would have been even higher if not for the dismal record of agricultural production in Africa.

The famine in Africa emphasizes the urgency of modernizing African agriculture. Fortunately, much of the required technology is presently available. The coupling of technology with economic incentives can increase agricultural output in Africa just as it has in many countries throughout the world.

There is no easy or quick solution to world hunger or economic development. Production of food and other products is limited by available resources, and the only realistic goal in any country is to make the most efficient use of these resources. The only effective way of increasing incomes is to increase capital formation and productivity. Foreign aid is no substitute for voluntary savings by the millions of people living in low-income countries.

Programs and policies affecting physical inputs will have little effect on output in the absence of the proper social and economic climate. Political controls of agriculture and other sectors of the economy inevitably stifle individual initiative, capital accumulation, and productivity. It is no accident that every country that has launched experiments in collectivized agriculture has witnessed a decrease in agricultural productivity. Hong Kong, Singapore, South Korea, and Taiwan are examples of countries that have prospered by shunning collectivist economic policies. The effect of recent limited privatization measures on agricultural output in China provides another dramatic example of the effect of economic incentives.

Increases in agricultural technology present a challenge to highly developed as well as to less developed countries. The temptation by government officials in both cases is to "manage agriculture." In the developed countries, domestic farm product prices are increased above competitive levels by expensive farm programs. Surpluses acquired in the operation of price support programs are often "dumped" in less developed countries. These policies are inimical to food production in less developed countries and to economic progress.

Rising farm productivity throughout the world now holds the promise of undermining these protectionist farm policies. There seems little doubt that farm producers in all countries will face more competition in domestic and foreign markets as currently available technology is adopted more widely. There is no way to determine now what the ultimate effects of these developments on world agriculture will be. We can be confident, however, that a more productive agriculture holds the potential to improve the lot of the world's hungry people. The challenge to governments in developed and less developed countries then is to abstain from policies that restrict competition and trade. Such restrictions prevent farmers and other workers in all countries from engaging in those activities in which they are most productive. Only through widespread use of decentralized competitive markets can agricultural resources throughout the world be used most productively, yielding maximum benefits to people in all countries.

1. The productivity figures cited in this section are from two papers by Dennis T. Avery, Senior Agricultural Analyst, Bureau of Intelligence and Research, U.S. Department of State. "The Dilemma of Rising Farm Productivity" was presented before The Agribusiness Roundtable, September 10, 1984. "The Bad News for Farmers Is That the Global Bad News Is Wrong" was presented before the N.C. Society of Farm Managers and Rural Appraisers, February 28, 1985.

2. "Business Brief: In Praise of Peasants," *The Economist*, February 2, 1985, pp. 86–87.

3. *Ibid*, p. 87.

4. *Ibid.*

5. "Peasants Rising," *The Economist*, February 2, 1985, pp. 11–12.

6. Dennis Avery, 1985, *op. cit.*, p. 3.

7. Dennis Avery, 1984, *op. cit.*, pp. 6–7.

8. Dennis Avery, 1985, *op. cit.*, p. 4.

9. P.T. Bauer, *Dissent on Development*, Revised ed. (Cambridge, Mass.: Harvard Univ. Press, 1976), pp. 95–132.

10. Ludwig von Mises, *Human Action* (Chicago: Henry Regnery and Co., 1966), p. 669.

11. Dennis Avery, 1985, *op. cit.*, p. 3.

8

Protectionism and Unemployment

by Hans F. Sennholz

In this article, Dr. Hans F. Sennholz addresses one of the major criticisms of a policy of free trade, its feared impact on unemployment. There is, says Dr. Sennholz, "a neomercantilism of the 1970s and 1980s" that is not as overtly nationalistic as the old mercantilism, but is "saturated with the notions and doctrines of full employment by government fiat." This neomercantilist position holds that the industrial nations would suffer widespread unemployment without such interferences in the marketplace as restrictions on imports, restrictions on the international movement of capital, and restrictions on immigration.

Dr. Sennholz examines a number of views associated with this position, for instance, the argument that free trade is only advantageous between countries that have the same standard of living, and finds them to be fallacious. He concludes that mass unemployment is a "self-inflicted evil" brought on primarily by the demands of labor organizations for government protection. Trade barriers are not a solution; they are a major cause of unemployment. Dr. Sennholz is the Chairman of the Economics Department at Grove City College in Pennsylvania and the author of more than 400 articles and books. This essay originally appeared in The Freeman *in March, 1985.*

There is a disturbing thing about foreign affairs: they are foreign. They do not conform to the world we admire, which is our own. Foreign matters are viewed with suspicion, yea, even dislike and contempt. Protectionism, which proposes to use the authority of government and its instruments of coercion to restrict trade with foreigners, builds on this psychological foundation.

In the minds of many people the ancient association of foreigner with enemy still lingers. Foreigners are blamed for all kinds of evil, real and imagined. They are censured for being inscrutable and unpredictable in their trade relations, engaging in ruthless competition, gouging their trade partners through prices too high or too low, exploiting their workers through sweatshop wages and conditions. But above all, trade with foreigners is believed to be most disruptive to commerce and industry, ever changing in composition and structure, requiring painful readjustment.

Protectionists offer instant gains through removal of foreign competition and protection from the pains of readjustment. Appealing to people who do not care to change and others who uphold domestic changes, but are set at odds with foreign changes, they promise peace and profit through legislation, regulation and the use of police power. But despite all the opposition to change, the world is a scene of changes. Today is not yesterday. We ourselves change as do our thoughts and works. Change may be painful, yet ever needful.

In our economic lives we may face important changes that require our attention and adjustment. The tastes, habits, choices and preferences of consumers may change, which may dictate production adjustments. The world-wide pattern of division of labor may change, which affects the structure of trade and commerce. The costs of production may change either here or abroad, which may create competitive advantages or disadvantages. There may be a never-ending sequence of changes in labor costs, capital costs, material costs, transportation costs, government costs, and many other costs.

Man faces changes in international trade and commerce to which he must adjust. After all, foreign trade is merely an extension of domestic trade, which is a corollary from the principles of division of labor. Cooperation and specialization bring the same kinds of benefits to all people regardless of race, religion or nationality. They make human labor more productive through exchange rather than direct production. If trade between the people in California, Texas, Florida, and Maine is advantageous, it follows that free trade between people in Guatemala and Mexico, or Canada and Costa Rica may also be advantageous.[1]

Protectionism, Old and New

Most of the arguments in favor of restriction stem from the distant past. Many are crudely mercantilistic; they favor exports and oppose imports. Mercantilists are concerned about an unfavorable balance of trade which, they believe, inflicts loss and waste. In the past they restricted imports and promoted exports in order to bring money into the country. The neomercantilists of our time favor exports for bringing in jobs and profits, and oppose imports for taking them out.

Mercantilistic notions, although discarded by most economists, live on regardless of the criticism that is levied against them. Businessmen remember them when they are encountering difficulties and calling on government, pleading protection from foreign competitors. The agents of labor retreat to the armory of mercantilism when they are enmeshed in depression and unemployment. And government officials may plead the case for mercantilism when they impose their regulations and controls on foreign trade and commerce, or grant subsidies, set rates, or gather information to promote exports and limit imports. They all hold to the persistent belief that exports are especially beneficial and praiseworthy, and imports *ipso facto* harmful.

The recrudescence of mercantilism dates back to the early part of this century, and came to a head during the 1930s. Guided by a spirit of nationalism it sought national self-sufficiency through restrictive tariffs, import quotas, and exchange restrictions. It differed from the older mercantilism in that it received strength and support from a philosophy of militant nationalism and economic welfarism. It was associated with comprehensive central planning by powerful governments engaging in economic warfare and military struggle.

The neomercantilism of the 1970s and 1980s differs from the 1930s' version in two important respects: it is devoid of the blatant nationalism of the first half of the century and its beggar-my-neighbor attitude; but it is saturated with the notions and doctrines of full employment by government fiat. Mindful of international sensibilities, it resorts to more subtle but equally deadly restrictions, to subsidies rather than tariffs and quotas. It does not aim at economic autarky for nationalistic ends, but at income and employment in favored industries. It does not spring from international confrontation, but from an inter-industry conflict that pits some industries against all others.

In the American steel industry, for example, capital and labor together conspire to restrict imports in order to boost corporate earnings and labor benefits. Embarassed by the low rates of production and the high rates of unemployment, they both call on government to restrain competition in any shape or form. They both plead as ardently for minimum wage legislation, which is designed to handicap other industries, as they argue forcefully against the competition of foreigners. For labor unions especially, government protection is of crucial importance. After all, to win substantial boosts in wages and benefits and subsequently suffer from staggering unemployment is casting serious doubt on the rationale of unionism.

Workers' Rights Movements in Europe and the U.S.A.

The labor movement in the U.S. closely resembles the workers' rights movements in the European welfare states. They both expound the doctrine that workers have an inherent right to a job, in their particular industry, at their present location and at rates of pay that exceed the market rates. To secure their right, government is expected to restrain foreign competition in any possible way and, if needed, subsidize both labor and capital.[2] In this respect, protectionism is a symptom of relatively weak national governments catering to powerful domestic interest groups, especially labor.

Protectionism also draws strength and support from the Keynesian mandate that government is responsible for full employment and that it must use its fiscal powers in a contracyclical manner. Such use of powers for purposes of market intervention may necessitate protection from foreign competition. After all, Keynesian recipes are national recipes that differ from those for world markets and international division of labor.

When Keynesian efforts succeed in raising goods prices, domestic producers suffer in competitiveness at home and abroad. Threatened by foreign competition, they may call for protection through import restrictions. When Keynesian efforts fail to achieve full employment the Keynesian planners further express their faith in government intervention as they turn to protectionist measures. The failure of Keynesianism breeds protectionism. Many Keynesians are joining the workers' rights movement and lending new luster to the promises of protection.[3]

Old Notions in New Garb

The labor movement and its Keynesian allies like to parade as champions of the less-developed countries. They are quick to disburse foreign aid to any and all applicants and finance their schemes of government enterprise. But many immediately draw the line when jobs are "exported" for the benefit of foreigners. They are dead set against capital and labor mobility that permits capital to move to less-developed countries and labor to more productive countries.[4] In all such matters they plead for restrictions that are said to bestow net benefits on society.

Man often errs through selfishness. Economic restrictions always benefit some people at the expense of others, and inflict net losses on society. Protectionists do not look beyond the range of direct involvement and dealing. American steel workers may see only their own wages and benefits which trade restrictions are meant to protect. They point at the market of goods and services catering to the steel industry in general and to steel workers in particular, and warn of dire consequences if these markets be permitted to decline. They completely ignore all other consequences and ramifications of restrictions, and refuse to admit that any favor bestowed on the steel industry is a disfavor to all others. Domestic trade is substituted for foreign trade, and domestic steel for foreign steel. The quantity of steel offered in exchange for other goods is reduced, which makes economic society universally poorer. The sellers of food, clothing, housing, education, and the like receive less steel in exchange for their goods and services. They would have been better off if they had been permitted to trade with foreign steel makers.

The protection argument for full employment is similar to that for net benefits.

To working people it seems self-evident that import restrictions add to the demand for labor and that steel and automobile quotas provide employment for steel and auto workers. Such evidence, unfortunately, is rather shallow and deceptive; it fails to consider other effects that are bound to follow. Import restrictions are restraints imposed by politicians and enforced by the apparatus of coercion, the courts and police. They constitute the use of brute force against people who voluntarily and peacefully are engaged in international exchange, in order to force them to act in a way they would not act if they were free.

Methods of Restriction Are Widely Available

The methods of restriction may vary greatly, from monetary exactions to outright confiscation of private property; they are highly effective in setting bounds to human action. When trade restrictions are imposed, the protected industry may temporarily enjoy special gains, which may cause it to expand and hire more labor, or retain more labor than it otherwise would. But this extra demand for labor, for instance, steel labor, is marred by a simultaneous decline in the demand for other labor, e.g., for food, clothing, housing. After all, the extra money spent on steel and steel products cannot be spent on other products, and the economic resources employed in the production of steel cannot be employed in other production. And the labor needed for the production of steel is no longer available for the production of food, clothing, housing, and so on.

At this point protectionists are quick to object that there is always unemployed labor and capital waiting to be called provided government lends a helping hand by restraining foreign competition. They point at mass unemployment in basic industries, such as steel, autos, mining, and transportation, and demand immediate correction through protection.

Unemployment undoubtedly is a great social evil that concerns us all. It is an economic phenomenon of loss and waste that harms not only the jobless but also their fellow workers who are forced to support them. In time it tends to turn into a political issue that breeds confrontation and conflict. To alleviate the evils of unemployment becomes an important political task. But it also raises the basic question of the suitability of the policies that are to create employment. In particular, it poses the question: can tariff barriers and other trade restrictions raise the demand for labor and alleviate the evils of unemployment?

Unemployment is a cost and wage phenomenon; foreign trade is exchange by individuals separated by political boundaries. The former is a manifestation of the law of price, which rests on the valuations by all members of society; the latter pertains to the scope of the division of labor which man is willing to practice. This scope does affect goods prices, including the price of labor. Improvements in the division of labor generally raise labor productivity and wage rates; deterioration reduces them. When government imposes trade restrictions it reduces the marginal productivity of labor and thereby lowers wage rates. If, in this situation, workers should refuse to suffer wage cuts, they are inviting mass unemployment. When seen in this light, trade barriers are effective instruments for causing unemployment.

In many respects production restrictions and trade barriers are like natural obstacles that thwart human effort and impair man's productivity. They both may increase the demand for specific labor. Destruction of housing by war, flood, earthquake or fire increases the demand for housing material and construction labor. But it also reduces the demand for a myriad of other goods which the destruction victims now must forgo. Similarly, import restrictions on steel may boost the demand for domestic steel, but they also reduce the demand for other goods which the restriction victims, that is, consumers must forgo. Steel producers and their workers may benefit from the new barriers; but the producers and workers in all other industries are likely to suffer losses.

Many workingmen welcome trade restrictions in the same way as they greet the breakdown and destruction of labor-saving tools and appliances. They are aware of the demand for their particular kind of labor and know how to increase it through protection and elimination of labor-saving tools. They apply the particular to the general and conclude that protection provides employment and destruction creates jobs. Unfortunately, they fail to see that both, restriction and destruction, are bound to reduce the marginal productivity of labor throughout the labor market. If, in this situation, affected workers should resist a prompt reduction of wage rates, which organized labor is likely to support with conviction and force, they face mass unemployment. After all, when the cost of labor exceeds its productivity, unemployment always makes its appearance.

Trade Restrictions Offer Temporary Relief

Trade restrictions may temporarily create new employment opportunities for a protected industry while other industries are forced to contract. But even in the protected industry they do not provide long-term employment, as the root causes of unemployment continue to be at work. The basic industries suffering from stagnation and unemployment generally are unionized industries with wages and benefits far in excess of nonunion market compensation. Labor unions enforce their rates through restriction of labor competition; the basic effect is unemployment. They apply their unrelenting pressures until they are enmeshed in depression and unemployment. To come to their rescue and grant them protection from foreign competition is to invite new restriction and more unemployment.

In a profound study, M. Kreinin recently demonstrated that labor compensation in the American automobile industry, in 1982, amounted to some 165 per cent of that in all manufactures. To become competitive with Japanese car makers, he concluded, United Auto Workers' compensation would have to fall by 24 per cent, which would leave their compensation still 25 per cent above the U.S. manufacturing average. Similarly, in iron and steel production, workers' wages and benefits amount to 189 per cent of those in all manufactures. To restore competitiveness with Japan they would have to fall by 39 per cent, which would leave their compensation still 15 per cent above the U.S. manufacturing average.[5] But no such solution to the chronic unemployment in the steel and auto industries is under consideration. Instead, their spokesmen are clamoring even louder for protection from "unfair" foreign competition.

Trade barriers destroy more jobs than they create. And yet, they have retained their popularity because most workers are convinced that they safeguard wage rates from the competition of low-cost labor. Without trade barriers, many Americans believe, foreign products made by cheap labor would flood the markets and force American labor to suffer substantial wage cuts or face unemployment. Free trade is said to be advantageous only between countries that have similar wage rates and similar standards of living, but thought to be harmful to people with high wages trading with people earning less. Americans and Canadians can trade with each other because they are similar in income and living conditions; but they must not trade with Mexicans who engage in unfair pauper-labor competition and cause U.S. living conditions to fall.

There are few arguments in favor of protection that are more popular and yet so specious and fallacious. When carried to its logical conclusion the wage-rate argument bars all trade across political boundaries as no two countries are identical in labor productivity and income. U.S. wage rates are generally higher than Canadian rates, which would call for American government protection from low-cost labor competition in Canada. Labor conditions may differ from state to state, yea, from community to community. Wage rates in New York state are generally higher than in Maine and Mississippi, which would call for government intervention in favor of labor in New York.

Differences in Productivity and Income Lead to Trade

In freedom, differences in labor productivity and income lead to exchanges of goods and services. As individual inequality brings forth man's division of labor so does his inequality in national productivity and output lead to international division of labor and goods exchanges. Adam Smith already taught that it is advantageous for a country to specialize in the production of those goods in which it has a cost advantage. David Ricardo added the law of comparative cost according to which it also is advantageous to a country to specialize in those items in which it has a comparative advantage.

To reap the advantages of an international division of labor a country may concentrate on production with greatest comparative advantage, importing even some items that can be produced at lower cost at home than abroad.[6] Improvements in international division of labor raise labor productivity and, wherever institutional restrictions have created unemployment, may actually lift some labor over the threshold of employability and thereby create jobs.

The competitive position of an industry may depend on the capital-labor composition of the product. A labor-intensive product, such as a hand-embroidered tablecloth, may be manufactured most advantageously in a low-wage country. A capital-intensive product requiring the application of large sums of capital may be manufactured most efficiently in the country with the largest per capita supply of capital and lowest interest rates. The manufacturers of Hong Kong, where wage rates are rather low when compared with U.S. standards, have a clear advantage in the production of hand-embroidery; U.S. manufacturers who benefit from efficient capital markets and relatively low capital costs have a clear cost advantage in the manufacture of capital-intensive products, for instance, $50-million airplanes.

Trade advantages may change when factor costs change. Where capital is being formed and made available at ever lower interest cost, capital-intensive industries are likely to prosper and expand. Where society and its political institutions consume productive capital, the industries can be expected to contract and discharge labor. When Toyota may secure capital for modernization and expansion at 7 per cent while General Motors is forced to pay 14 per cent in a depleted capital market, it becomes rather obvious that Toyota will continue to expand and employ more labor while GM must be expected to contract and dismiss some labor.

Many Factors Affect the Degree of Competition

The costs of capital and labor are merely two of many factors that determine the competitiveness of an industry. There are many other factors such as the methods of production and the state of technology, transportation costs for materials and supplies and for products to their markets, government regulation, taxation, environmental costs and other institutional costs. A change of any one, at home or abroad, may materially alter the competitive position of an industry. The formation of capital per head of the population generally raises labor productivity and reduces unemployment; the consumption of capital lowers labor productivity and depresses wage rates. Where labor resists the reduction and insists on remuneration that exceeds market rates, it invites mass unemployment.

It is significant that governments generally do not protect industries with relatively low rates of productivity and wages, industries with a great deal of unskilled labor. In the U.S. these industries are forced to labor under great difficulties created by minimum wage legislation. The U.S. government, under the influence of powerful labor interests, apparently prefers foreign imports from low-wage countries such as Korea, Hong Kong, and Taiwan over domestic production in the South and especially Puerto Rico. But it is granting considerable protection to industries that are known to pay the highest wage rates in the world.

The U.S. government is guided by the doctrine of ''no injury,'' which brought into being the ''escape clause'' where injury is reported, and the ''peril points'' below which import duties must not be reduced. Protectionism is visible in the trade adjustment assistance granted to workers, in agreements with foreign exporters, the establishment of the International Trade Commission, and other concessions granted to interests with congressional clout. Protectionism springs ever anew from the efforts of ''distributional coalitions,'' which use political power to restrict competition and output.

U.S.-Japanese Trade Relations

Protectionists in the U.S. spend a great deal of time and effort worrying and complaining about Japanese trade practices. They focus their concern on Japan with which the United States is running a huge deficit in its merchandise trade account. According to the Council of Economic Advisers *Annual Report*, the 1976–83 deficit amounted to some $95 billion primarily as a result of Japanese sales of textiles, television sets, automobiles, motorcycles, radios, photographic equipment, video tape recorders, watches, machine tools, and steel.[7] A *Business Week* cover story calls it ''America's Hidden Problem: The Huge Trade Deficit is Sapping Growth and Exporting Jobs.'' (August 29, 1983).

American complaints about Japanese trade practices may have some merit, but they do not lead to the conclusions drawn by *Business Week* and other protectionists. They do not justify making Japan the ''whipping boy'' for trade deficits for which the U.S. government is primarily responsible. After all, it is an undeniable fact that U.S. trade restrictions completely bar Japanese buyers from important U.S. markets and thereby inflict visible losses not only on American producers but also on the Japanese people as consumers. Trade deficits may spring from a number of causes among which disruptive policies conducted by the U.S. government must not be overlooked.

There is transcendent power in example. U.S. leadership in international policy-making may be slipping because the U.S. example is unconvincing. The U.S. surely is no free-trade country; the U.S. government has entered into international trade agreements on cocoa, coffee, rubber, sugar, and tea. It has built trigger price mechanisms in steel and imposed ''voluntary'' quotas on autos and textiles. The maritime industry represented by seamen's unions and unionized domestic shipbuilders has managed to obtain legislation that forces Alaskan oil producers to ship their products in high-cost U.S. tankers to uneconomic destinations in the U.S. The legislation hit hard at Japanese levels of living by cutting the Japanese people off from Alaskan crude oil. It is estimated that, under free-trade conditions, they could be expected to buy some $15 billion annually, which alone would eliminate the merchandise trade deficit with Japan.[8]

The Japanese people must import almost all of their oil. In a free world unhampered by trade barriers Alaskan producers would be their least-cost suppliers. In the political world of trade restrictions special interests in the U.S. deny them access to the Alaskan market. The Trans-Alaska Pipeline Authorization Act of 1973 and the 1977 and 1979 amendments to the Export Administration Act virtually shut the Alaskan door to foreigners and forced them to seek supplies in far-distant Arabian and African markets. It is obvious that transport charges per barrel of Saudi oil are substantially higher than for Alaskan oil, and materially higher for Alaskan oil shipped to the West Coast and the Gulf Coast than for oil shipped to Japan.

Higher Shipping Costs

The higher transportation costs visibly raise total cost, which increases world prices, reduces labor productivity and impairs economic well-being. But a few American seamen and shipbuilders are enjoying a windfall through trade disruption. It is estimated that more than 90 per cent of U.S. shipping capacity, measured in deadweight tonnage, and probably more than half of all American seamen serve to carry oil from Alaska to U.S. ports.[9]

Notions of full employment and favors to organized labor have led the U.S. government to impose an embargo not only on the shipment of Alaskan crude but also on the sale of timber to Japan. There are 20,000 saw mills in Japan, supplying housing and furnishings for 120 million people, but U.S. legislation passed in 1968 practically bars them from American markets. It bans exports of unfinished logs cut on Federally owned land, which amount to some 65 per cent of the softwood sawtimber inventory in the U.S., and dictates that all such logs must be processed prior to export. The law even prohibits "substitution," that is, the purchase of Federal timber by American merchants who export timber cut on private lands.[10]

Surely, such measures neither reduce the U.S. merchandise trade deficit with Japan nor improve U.S.-Japanese relations. And yet, they continue to spring forth from the primitive notion that the log export ban forces foreigners to purchase finished products and thereby provides employment to wood processors and furniture makers. Fortunately, political force does not produce sales and employment; both obey only the laws of the market. The timber legislation actually has reduced employment in the American timber industry and prevents employment in cutting and shipping timber to Japan. It serves to reduce the marginal productivity of labor, to lower wage rates in both the U.S. and Japan and, wherever labor resists the downward pressure, contributes to mass unemployment. It puts the misunderstood interest of a powerful special-interest group ahead of national interest and gives much ammunition to the neomercantilists who are fretting about the merchandise trade imbalances.

"Buy American"

There are many more U.S. barriers to trade with Japan and other countries. The most noticeable probably are "Buy American" statutes that give preference to domestic products in Federal and state government contracts. Federal agencies are required to pay up to 6 per cent more for products made in the U.S. The Federal aid program to mass transit systems requires that only American materials be used. The foreign aid program requires that at least 50 per cent of the gross tonnage of all commodities thus financed be carried by American flag vessels. At least 18 states restrict the use of foreign steel and aluminum and order the purchase of domestic products. Many require state bids to carry a clause restricting the use of foreign materials and calling for American-made products. Many local authorities enact building codes that ban the use of foreign materials.

Countless Federal statutes and regulations prevent or limit imports of agricultural products such as beef, dairy produce, mandarin oranges, and sugar. In recent years the U.S. government sought voluntary restraints of foreign sales, which were as voluntary as a judge's temporary restraining order. In recent months it finally dispensed with the pretense of voluntarism. Protection from foreign competition now covers all basic industries that are forced to compete in U.S. markets. Its costs to American consumers in the form of higher goods prices amount to many billions of dollars. A recent study estimated the 1980 costs at more than $58 billion, or $255 per American consumer.[11] They probably have more than doubled since then. Its costs to American workers in the form of lower labor productivity and higher rates of unemployment can only be surmised.

The pressures for protection from foreign competition continue to grow in the U.S. and other countries. Well-organized groups, especially organized labor, use the political apparatus to reap economic gains through political force. Unable to compete effectively and suffering from depression and unemployment, for which they deny all responsibility, they seek refuge with government and its coercive powers. They noisily demand protection from foreign competition that is held responsible for their plight. Economists do know, however, that mass unemployment, no matter how painful it may be, cannot be placed on the doorsteps of foreigners. It is a self-inflicted evil of radical interventionism that cannot be alleviated by beggar-thy-neighbor policies. Protectionism only exacerbates it.

1. Cf. theoretical works: Gottfried Haberler, *The Theory of International Trade* (London: Hodge, [1933] 1936); also his *Survey of International Trade Theory*, Rev. and enl. edition, (Princeton University International Finance Section, [1954] 1961); James E. Meade, *The Theory of International Economic Policy*, Vol. 2; *Trade and Welfare* (New York: Oxford University Press, 1955); Ragnar Nurkse, *Problems of Capital Formation in Underdeveloped Countries* (New York: Oxford University Press, [1953] 1962); Jacob Viner, *Studies in the Theory of International Trade* (New York: Harper, 1937); Leland B. Yeager, and David G. Tuerck, *Foreign Trade and U.S. Policy: The Case for Free International Trade* (New York: Praeger Publishers, 1976). Cf. also the classical historical work of Frank W. Taussig, *The Tariff History of the United States* (New York: Putnam, [1888] 1931).

2. See Melvyn B. Krauss, "Ill Fares the Welfare State," *Policy Review* 18 (Fall 1981), pp. 133–38; also *The New Protectionism: The Welfare State and International Trade* (New York: New York University Press, 1978).

3. Robert B. Reich, "Beyond Free Trade," *Foreign Affairs* 61 (Spring 1983), pp. 773–804; Bob Kuttner, "The Free Trade Fallacy," *New Republic*, 28 March 1983, pp. 16–21; G. William Miller, ed., *Regrowing the American Economy* (Englewood Cliffs, N.J.: Prentice-Hall, 1983); Leonard Silk, *The Economists*, (New York: Avon Books, 1978); see also *Allied Industrial Worker*, Official Newspaper of the Allied Industrial Workers of America (AFL-CIO) International Union, Milwaukee, Wisc., September, 1984; *CWA News*, Communication Workers of America, AFL-CIO, Washington, D.C., September 1984.

4. See Melvyn B. Krauss, *Development Without Aid* (New York: MaGraw-Hill, 1983), especially Chapter 7.

5. Mordechai E. Kreinin, "Wage Competitiveness in the U.S. Auto and Steel Industries," *Contemporary Policy Issues* 4 (January 1984), pp. 39–50.

6. Cf. David Ricardo, *Works and Correspondence*, Edited by Piero Sraffa (Cambridge University Press, 1951–1955), Vol. I, *On the Principles of Political Economy and Taxation*.

7. Council of Economic Advisers, *Annual Report* (Washington, D.C.: Government Printing Office, 1984).

8. Beth deHamel, James R. Ferry, William W. Hogan, and Joseph S. Nie, Jr., *The Export of Alaskan Crude Oil: An Analysis of the Economic and National Security Benefits* (Cambridge, Mass.: Putnam, Hayes, and Bartlett, Inc., 1983).

9. Steve H. Hanke, "U.S.-Japanese Trade: Myth and Realities," *Cato Journal*, 3/3, Winter 1983/84, p. 762.

10. Barney Dowdle and Steve H. Hanke, "Public Timber Policy and the Wood-Products Industry." in *Forest Lands, Public and Private*, ed. M. Bruce Johnson and Robert Deacon (Cambridge, Mass.: Ballinger Publishing Co., 1984).

11. See Murray L. Weidenbaum, *Business, Government and the Public*, 2nd ed. (Englewood Cliffs, N.J.: Prentice-Hall, 1981), pp. 253–55; also "The High Cost of Protectionism," *Cato Journal, Ibid*, pp. 777–791.

Part Three

War and the Welfare State

T his section of the book analyzes further the part that the welfare state plays in twentieth-century international conflict. It was one thing to hold in the nineteenth century that trade restrictions are a primary cause of war, as both Frederic Bastiat in France and Richard Cobden in England independently concluded. The nineteenth century was a period of relative peace, in which classical liberal theorists could look back on a series of limited wars and look around them at a developing international division of labor, which they hoped would lead to the abolition of war.

But war has not been abolished. Instead, the twentieth century has replaced limited war by unlimited war. Wars are no longer fought by armies on battlefields; they involve entire populations. What has the classical liberal analysis to say about contemporary warfare?

The central argument in Part Three is that of Ludwig von Mises, who says that it was the replacement of laissez faire with the welfare state that required the replacement of limited with unlimited warfare. He analyzes how, after the international division of labor developed in the late nineteenth century, the price of government economic intervention went up. One nation's domestic economic restrictions affect the standard of living of people in other countries, making war not only more likely, but more total. Winning has become crucial for the general population. "If the tailor goes to war against the baker," Mises writes, "he must henceforth produce his bread for himself."

The remaining pieces carry aspects of the Mises argument further. David Osterfeld delves into two aspects of it—the line of causation from a minimum wage measure to protection against foreign competition, and the historical sequence from laissez faire under limited democracy to the welfare state, as politicians began promising more to an expanding suffrage. Hans F. Sennholz takes up the parallels in the domestic and foreign *modi operandi* of the welfare state, before speculating in some detail as to how national interests could be protected in a laissez-faire world. And, finally, Samuel H. Husbands illustrates the analysis with both economic and historical examples, ending with his policy suggestions on how the United States could protect its national interest through free trade.

9

The Economics of War

by Ludwig von Mises

Ludwig von Mises (1881–1973) was the leading member of the Austrian School of economic thought. He taught at the University of Vienna until 1934 and then at the Institute of International Studies in Geneva until 1940, when he emigrated to the United States, ultimately becoming a U.S. citizen. He taught at New York University from 1945 until his retirement in 1969. The most outstanding of his many publications was Human Action, *first published in English by Yale University Press in 1949 and later by Contemporary Books, Inc. This essay, a condensed excerpt from* Human Action, *was first published in its present form in* Ideas on Liberty #3, *in November 1955.*

Mises notes that, in early European civilization, unlimited dreams of conquest were limited by the fact that war was waged by rulers whose subjects had little stake in the outcome. As an international division of labor arose, it created the possibility of undreamed of prosperity, but it also made the ordinary citizen more dependent on foreign trade. Classical liberalism, especially as enunciated by the Manchester School in England, correctly identified that "the emergence of the international division of labor requires the total abolition of war." But instead, limited war was replaced by total war as laissez faire was replaced by the welfare state, creating "conflicts for which no peaceful solution can be found."

The market economy involves peaceful cooperation. It bursts asunder when the citizens turn into warriors and, instead of exchanging commodities and services, fight one another.

The wars fought by primitive tribes did not affect cooperation under the division of labor. Such cooperation by and large did not exist between the warring parties before the outbreak of hostilities. These wars were unlimited or total wars. They aimed at total victory and total defeat. The defeated were either exterminated or expelled from their dwelling places or enslaved. The idea that a treaty could settle the conflict and make it possible for both parties to live in peaceful neighborly conditions was not present in the minds of fighters.

The spirit of conquest does not acknowledge restraints other than those imposed by a power which resists successfully. The principle of empire building is to expand the sphere of supremacy as far as possible. The great Asiatic conquerors and the Roman Imperators were stopped only when they could not march further. Then they postponed aggression for later days. They did not abandon their ambitious plans and did not consider independent foreign states as anything else than targets for later onslaughts.

The philosophy of boundless conquest also animated the rulers of medieval Europe. They too aimed first of all at the utmost expansion of the size of their realms. But the institutions of feudalism provided them with only scanty means for warfare. Vassals were not obliged to fight for their lord more than a limited time. The selfishness of the vassals who insisted on their rights checked the king's aggressiveness. Thus the peaceful coexistence of a number of sovereign states originated. In the sixteenth century a Frenchman, Bodin, developed the theory of national sovereignty. In the seventeenth century a Dutchman, Grotius, added to it a theory of international relations in war and peace.

Mercenaries

With the disintegration of feudalism, sovereigns could no longer rely upon summoned vassals. They "nationalized" the country's armed forces. Henceforth, the warriors were the king's mercenaries. The organization, equipment, and support of such troops were rather costly and a heavy burden on the ruler's revenues. The ambitions of the princes were unbounded, but financial considerations forced them to moderate their designs. They no longer planned to conquer a whole country. All they aimed at was the conquest of a few cities or of a province. To attain more would also have been unwise politically. For the European powers were anxious not to let any one of them become too powerful and a menace to their own safety. A too impetuous conqueror must always fear a coalition of all those whom his bigness has frightened.

The combined effect of military, financial, and political circumstances produced the limited warfare which prevailed in Europe in the three hundred years preceding the French Revolution. Wars were fought by comparatively small armies of professional soldiers. War was not an affair of the peoples; it concerned the rulers only. The citizens detested war which brought mischief to them and burdened them with taxes and contributions. But they considered themselves victims of events in which they did not participate actively. Even the belligerent armies respected the "neutrality" of the civilians. As they saw it, they were fighting the supreme war lord of the hostile forces, but not the noncombatant subjects of the enemy. In the wars fought on the European continent the property of civilians was considered inviolable. In 1856 the Congress of Paris made an attempt to extend this principle to naval warfare. More and more, eminent minds began to discuss the possibility of abolishing war altogether.

Abolition of War

Looking at conditions as they had developed under the system of limited warfare, philosophers found wars useless. So they reasoned as follows: Men are killed or maimed, wealth is destroyed, countries are devastated for the sole benefit of kings and ruling oligarchies. The peoples themselves do not derive any gain from victory. The individual citizens are not enriched if their rulers expand the size of their realm by annexing a province. For the people wars do not pay. The only cause of armed conflict is the greed of autocrats. The substitution of representative government for royal despotism will abolish war altogether. Democracies are peaceful. It is no concern of theirs whether their nation's sovereignty stretches over a larger or smaller territory. They will treat territorial problems without bias and passion. They will settle them peacefully. What is needed to make peace durable is to dethrone the despots. This, of course, cannot be achieved peacefully. It is necessary to crush the mercenaries of the kings. But this revolutionary war of the peoples against the tyrants will be the last war, the war to abolish war forever.

This idea was already dimly present in the minds of the French revolutionary leaders when, after having repelled the invading armies of Prussia and Austria, they embarked upon a campaign of aggression. Of course, under the leadership of Napoleon they themselves very soon adopted the most ruthless methods of boundless expansion and annexation until a coalition of all European powers frustrated their ambitions. But the idea of durable peace was soon resurrected. It was one of the main points in the body of nineteenth-century liberalism as consistently elaborated in the much abused principles of the Manchester School.

These British liberals and their continental friends were keen enough to realize that what can safeguard durable peace is not simply government by the people, but government by the people under unlimited laissez faire. In their eyes free trade, both in domestic affairs and in international relations, was the necessary prerequisite of the preservation of peace. In such a world without trade and migration barriers no incentives for war and conquest are left. Fully convinced of the irrefutable persuasiveness of the liberal ideas, they dropped the notion of the last war to abolish all wars. All peoples will of their own accord recognize the blessings of free trade and peace and will curb their domestic despots without any aid from abroad.

Most historians entirely fail to recognize the factors which replaced the "limited" war of the "ancien régime" by the "unlimited" war of our age. As they see it, the change came with the shift from the dynastic to the national form of state and was a consequence of the French Revolution. They look only upon attending phenomena and confuse causes and effects. They speak of the composition of the armies, of strategical and tactical principles, weapons and transportation facilities, and of many other matters of military art and administrative technicalities.[1] However, all these things do not explain why modern nations prefer aggression to peace.

There is perfect agreement with regard to the fact that total war is an offshoot of aggressive nationalism. But this is merely circular reasoning. We call aggressive nationalism that ideology which makes for modern total war. Aggressive nationalism is the necessary derivative of the policies of intervention and national planning. While laissez faire eliminates the causes of international conflict, socialism and government interference with business create conflicts for which no peaceful solution can be found. While under free trade and freedom of migration no individual is concerned about the territorial size of his country, under the protective measures of economic nationalism nearly every citizen has a substantial interest in these territorial issues. The enlargement of the territory subject to the sovereignty of his own government means material improvement for him or at least relief from restrictions which a foreign government has imposed upon his well-being. What has transformed the limited war between royal armies into total war, the clash between peoples, is not technicalities of military art, but the substitution of the Welfare State for the laissez-faire state.

Lebensraum

If Napoleon I had reached his goal, the French Empire would have stretched far beyond the limits of 1815. Spain and Naples would have been ruled by kings of the house of Bonaparte-Murat instead of kings of another French family, the Bourbons. The palace of Kassel would have been occupied by a French playboy instead of one of the egregious Electors of the Hesse family. All these things would not have made the citizens of France more prosperous. Neither did the citizens of Prussia win anything from the fact that their king in 1866 evicted his cousins of Hanover, Hesse-Kassel, and Nassau from their luxurious residences. But if Hitler had realized his plans, the Germans expected to enjoy a higher standard of living. They were confident that the annihilation of the French, the Poles, and the Czechs would make every member of their own race richer. The struggle for more Lebensraum was their own war.

Under laissez faire peaceful coexistence of a multitude of sovereign nations is possible. Under government control of business it is impossible. The tragic error of President Wilson is that he ignored this essential point. Modern total war has nothing in common with the limited war of the old dynasties. It is a war against trade and migration barriers, a war of the comparatively overpopulated countries against the comparatively underpopulated. It is a war to abolish those institutions which prevent the emergence of a tendency toward an equalization of wage rates all over the world. It is a war of the farmers tilling poor soil against those governments which bar them from access to much more fertile soil lying fallow. It is, in short, a war of wage earners and farmers who describe themselves as underprivileged "have-nots" against wage earners and farmers of other nations whom they consider privileged "haves."

The acknowledgment of this fact does not suggest that victorious wars would really do away with those evils about which the aggressors complain. Neither does it mean that there can be any question of appeasing the aggressors by removing migration barriers. As conditions are today, the Americas and Australia in admitting German, Italian, and Japanese immigrants would merely open their doors to the vanguards of hostile armies.

It is futile to place confidence in treaties, conferences, and such bureaucratic outfits as the League of Nations and the United Nations. Plenopotentiaries, office clerks, and experts make a poor show in fighting ideologies. The spirit of conquest cannot be smothered by red tape. What is needed is a radical change in ideologies and economic policies. . . .

If an economically self-sufficient man starts a feud against another autarkic man, no specific problems of "war economy" arise. But if the tailor goes to war against the baker, he must henceforth produce his bread for himself. If he neglects to do this, he will be in distress sooner than his adversary, the baker. For the baker can wait longer for a new suit than the tailor can for fresh bread. The economic problem of making war is therefore different for the baker and for the tailor.

Free Trade and Peace

The international division of labor was developed under the assumption that there would no longer be wars. In the philosophy of the Manchester School free trade and peace were seen as mutually conditioning one another. The businessmen who made trade international did not consider the possibility of new wars arising. Nor did general staffs and students of the art of warfare pay any attention to the change in conditions which international division of labor brought about. The method of military science consists in examining the experience of wars fought in the past and in abstracting general rules from it. Even the most scrupulous occupation with the campaigns of Turenne and Napoleon I could not suggest the existence of a problem which was not present in ages in which there was practically no international division of labor.

The European military experts slighted the study of the American Civil War. In their eyes this war was not instructive. It was fought by armies of irregulars led by nonprofessional commanders. Civilians like Lincoln interfered with the conduct of the operations. Little, they believed, could be learned from his experience. But it was in the Civil War that, for the first time, problems of the interregional division of labor played the decisive role. The South was predominantly agricultural, its processing industries were negligible. The Confederates depended on the supply of manufacturers from Europe. As the naval forces of the Union were strong enough to blockade their coast, they soon began to lack needed equipment.

The Germans in both World Wars had to face the same situation. They depended on the supply of foodstuffs and raw materials from overseas. But they could not run the British blockade. In both wars the outcome was decided by the battles of the Atlantic. The Germans lost because they failed in their efforts to cut off the British Isles from access to the world market and could not themselves safeguard their own maritime supply lines. The strategical problem was determined by the conditions of the international division of labor. . . .

Advantages of Cooperation

What distinguishes man from animals is the insight into the advantages that can be derived from cooperation under the division of labor. Man curbs his innate instinct of aggression in order to cooperate with other human beings. The more he wants to improve his material well-being, the more he must expand the system of the division of labor. Concomitantly, he must more and more restrict the sphere in which he resorts to military action. The emergence of the international division of labor requires the total abolition of war. Such is the essence of the laissez-faire philosophy of Manchester.

This philosophy is, of course, incompatible with statolatry. In its context the State, the social apparatus of violent oppression, is entrusted with the protection of the smooth operation of the market economy against the onslaughts of antisocial individuals and gangs. Its function is indispensable and beneficial, but it is an ancillary function only. There is no reason to idolize the police power and ascribe to it omnipotence and omniscience. There are things which it can certainly not accomplish. It cannot conjure away the scarcity of the factors of production, it cannot make people more prosperous, it cannot raise the productivity of labor. All it can achieve is to prevent gangsters from frustrating the efforts of those people who are intent upon promoting material well-being.

The liberal philosophy of Bentham and Bastiat had not yet completed its work of removing trade barriers and government meddling with business when the counterfeit theology of the divine state began to take effect. Endeavors to improve the conditions of wage earners and small farmers by government decree made it necessary to loosen more and more the ties which connected each country's domestic economy with those of other countries. Economic nationalism, the necessary complement of domestic interventionism, hurts the interests of foreign peoples and thus creates international conflict. It suggests the idea of amending this unsatisfactory state of affairs by war. Why should a powerful nation tolerate the challenge of a less powerful nation? Is it not insolence on the part of small Lapputania to injure the citizens of big Ruritania by customs, migration barriers, foreign exchange control, quantitative trade restrictions, and expropriation of Ruritanian investments in Lapputania? Would it not be easy for the army of Ruritania to crush Lapputania's contemptible forces?

Such was the ideology of the German, Italian, and Japanese warmongers. It must be admitted that they were consistent from the point of view of the new "unorthodox" teachings. Interventionism generates economic nationalism, and economic nationalism generates bellicosity. If men and commodities are prevented from crossing the borderlines, why should not the armies try to pave the way for them? . . .

Modern civilization is a product of the philosophy of laissez faire. It cannot be preserved under the ideology of government omnipotence. . . . To defeat the aggressors is not enough to make peace durable. The main thing is to discard the ideology that generates war.

1. The best presentation of the traditional interpretation is provided by the book, *Makers of Modern Strategy, Military Thought from Machiavelli to Hitler*, ed. E. M. Earle (Princeton University Press, 1944); cf. especially the contribution of R. R. Palmer, pp. 49–53.

10

The Nature of
Modern Warfare

by David Osterfeld

*Contrary to uninformed opinion, it is not capitalism that causes wars, says
David Osterfeld, but government intervention. Dr. Osterfeld is an associate
professor of political science at St. Joseph's College in Rensselaer, Indiana, and
also a Fellow of the Institute for Humane Studies at George Mason University. In
this essay that first appeared in* The Freeman *of April 1972, he cites Pitirim
Sorokin's analysis of 1000 wars over a period of 25 centuries, and Sorokin's
conclusion that, of all the centuries examined, the twentieth is the "bloodiest and
most belligerent."*

*How can this be, since the twentieth century saw the rise of economic
intervention, and most economic intervention has humanitarian aims? The effect
of a specific intervention—minimum wage laws—is then examined in detail to
show how such welfarism does increase the likelihood of war. Osterfeld points
out that there are only three ways to "procure the necessities of life": by
producing them, by trading for them, or by taking them by force. Exports must
equal imports, and the international division of labor requires that a nation must
import at least some necessities. This being so, when the prices of exports or
imports are raised noncompetitively—by domestic welfarism or by foreign
tariffs—the nation's ultimate recourse is to try to fill its needs by conquest, as
Adolf Hitler did. Dr. Osterfeld concludes his argument by linking the rise of
welfarism to the desire of politicians to woo new voting populations with
benefits, as the suffrage was extended to more and more groups.*

I n reflecting upon the intensity of the sentiment and the methods utilized in
contemporary antiwar protests, it seems manifest that the preference is
always for peace; that nobody wants war. So, one must ask why, if no one
wants war, do wars continue to occur?

Perhaps wars result, not from the direct intentions of "war-mongering capitalists" or any other group for that matter, but as Edmund Opitz observed, they are the "unexpected by-product," the inevitable culmination, of particular political or economic policies not intended to be aggressive and, in fact, even humanitarianly motivated. What one must, therefore, attempt to discern is the generic nature of these particular policies whose underlying elements propel us toward war. Only if we are cognizant of the processes that cause wars can we ever hope to obviate these warlike tendencies.

The crux of this thesis, however, is nearly diametrically opposed to today's prevailing ethos which attempts to explain war, more often than not, as the result of the insidious machinations of the industrial magnates or the "warmongering capitalists," or insists that by its nature the capitalist system must culminate in violent conflicts and, ultimately, its own catastrophic demise. The position here is to equate classical liberalism and capitalism with peace rather than war. Conversely, it considers the factors begetting war as endemic, not in socialism per se, but in any type of government economic intervention of which socialism is merely one form.

Aggressive Nationalism Follows Intervention

While everyone is agreed that the cause of war is aggressive nationalism, the position here is that aggressive nationalism is the necessary outcome of government intervention. In other words, statism fosters nationalism. An in-depth study of nearly 1000 wars fought in the West from 500 B. C. to A. D. 1925 was conducted by the sociologist, Pitirim Sorokin. In contrasting the size of the casualty list to the corresponding population, he determined that the war magnitude of the first quarter of the twentieth century stood at 52 per 1,000,000 (compared with 17 for the nineteenth century) leading Sorokin to conclude that "the twentieth century will unquestionably prove to be the bloodiest and most belligerent of all the twenty-five centuries under consideration."[1]

These figures are in accord with the two salient contentions of this article. If a general date can be given for the beginning of the abandonment of the principles of laissez faire for those of government intervention and control, it would be the 1870s, highlighted by events such as Germany's appointment of Bismarck as Chancellor and the emergence of the first effects of Britain's Reform Bill of 1867. Since that time, the trend has been conspicuously away from limited democracy and laissez faire and toward government economic interference. We can say, generally, that the age of classical liberalism was the nineteenth century and that the age of statism extends from the latter part of that century to the present.

In applying Dr. Sorokin's findings to that of our historical sketch, two things we have noted become manifest. On the one hand is the relative peace and tranquility enjoyed by a world embracing largely laissez-faire principles. On the other we see, with the substitution of the deification of the state and rise of the controlled economy for the principles of classical liberalism, the concomitant rise of war and international conflict.

The question to be considered now is why government intervention—whether it be socialism or a "mixed" or welfare economy, and whether for humanitarian or insidious purposes—engenders international conflicts and war.

Domestic Ramifications of Statism

The free market is perpetually heading toward equilibrium. Wages and prices are always heading toward a point at which the supply of laborers and of commodities equals the demand for them. Any attempt to interfere with the natural operation of market pricing is destined to engender economic imbalance, begetting in turn, international conflict.

To illustrate how this occurs, we will follow the linkage of events in any government interference. We will assume, moreover, that the intervention occurs under the most propitious circumstances; that it is, in other words, humanitarianly motivated. We will say, for example, that the government has intervened in an endeavor to raise the wages of the hardpressed or to set a minimum standard for the lowest strata of the working force. Surely, most would exclaim, this is a generous act; surely there could be nothing sinister or pernicious about such a policy; surely this would ease, not aggravate, tension. However, let's examine it more closely.

If wages are forced up, prices also may rise. Either they will rise nearly simultaneously, or the increased wages will reduce the income of the entrepreneurs, thus driving the marginal producers out of business and discouraging additional investment in those fields. This diminution in the amount of capital investment will entail a reduction in the quantity of commodities produced, thus causing prices to rise. And the same thing is true of endeavors to hold prices down. At the lower prices, more is bought. But the reduced price discourages investment and once again forces the marginal producers out of business, thereby engendering shortages that can only be corrected by either (1) removing the controls and permitting prices to rise or (2) carrying on production through means of subsidies, which requires higher prices in other fields. Any government intervention, therefore, must inevitably create imbalances in the economy; these, in turn, tend to bring a rise in production costs and therefore in prices.

This rise in prices, moreover, must have catastrophic international ramifications. Since domestic wages and prices are artificially held above the level set by the free market, the lower prices offered by imported goods will encourage the buying of the imported commodities in preference to domestically produced goods. As long as prices domestically are maintained at bloated levels, this foreign underselling ultimately will force the domestic firms out of business. Moreover, maintaining wages domestically above their respective equilibrium levels will attract immigrants from abroad. The influx of new laborers will either force the bloated wage level down or engender institutional mass unemployment.

The apparent solution for such problems is a policy of autarky, viz., economic isolation, as best manifested by recourse to tariff and migration barriers, exchange controls, and the like.

International Ramifications: War

It should now be evident that a country intent upon controlling wages and prices cannot permit either imports or immigration. Such penetration would easily and obviously frustrate the planners. Statism, therefore, becomes synonomous with autarky. With the possible exceptions of the U.S. and U.S.S.R., hardly any nation is adequately blessed with the means of self-sufficiency; statism and autarky, therefore, must manifest themselves as a policy of aggressive nationalism. As Lionel Robbins observed: "It is really ridiculous to suppose that such a policy is possible for the majority.. . . . To recommend autarky as a general policy is to recommend war as an instrument for making autarky possible."

It may be well to consider this passage further. In the long run, exports must always equal imports. The only reason one gives up an object in trade is to acquire that which he does not possess but values more than what he is giving up; similarly, the only need for exports is to pay for the required imports. Thus, the greater the imports demanded for subsistence, the greater the exports required to pay for them.

A nation, in endeavoring to preserve domestic wage and price increases through recourse to tariff and migration barriers, thereby eliminates the possibility of exporting its surplus commodities and thus acquiring the foreign exchange necessary to purchase imports. There are only three ways to procure the necessities of life: (1) to produce them at home, (2) to trade for them, or (3) to go to war and take them. If a nation does not possess the kind or the necessary quantities of natural resources, and if it does not possess enough fertile agricultural land to provide for its population, then it must trade for these necessities. If it erects tariff barriers and prohibits imports—or if other nations erect tariffs that prohibit exports—a nation is then unable to trade for its necessities. Unless one subscribes to the unlikely proposition that the people of one nation will passively acquiesce in permitting either starvation or a substantial reduction in their standard of living, there is only one recourse left: war.

World Wars I and II are replete with support for this hypothesis.[2] It is important to note that between the wars, for example, all European nations resorted to very strict anti-immigration laws, in most cases prohibiting immigration altogether. Every nation was eager to protect its wage level against enchroachment from nations with still lower wage levels. Such policies were bound to engender serious international friction.

Moreover, like the ''Sozialpolitik'' of pre-1914 Germany, Hitler's Germany endeavored to raise the wage rates of its workers. In doing so, prices were forced up. Since this would have encouraged imports and thus thwarted the statist schemes, tariff barriers were established. However, the German ban on imports meant that no nation could acquire the necessary German exchange to purchase German exports. Germany, an industrial nation, was largely dependent upon foreign foodstuffs. It had to export its industrial commodities in order to obtain much of the needed food. By eliminating imports, it eliminated, in a like degree, the only means by which it could peaceably attain these necessary agricultural and other products. So, Germany had but one alternative; it had to go to war and take them.

Rise of Aggressive Nationalism

The nineteenth century was governed largely by classical liberal principles. It was, for the most part, a peaceful century. The onslaught of war accompanied the abandonment of these principles. The question to be considered, therefore, is precisely why these policies were discarded. The answer can be perceived if one realizes that an integral element of this liberalism was democratic rule. It is imperative, however, to appreciate that this was the democracy of Tocqueville; that is, a limited democracy. Under the classical liberal ideal, the power of the state—the apparatus of compulsion and control—was severely circumscribed. The crux of this concept was the recognition of individual rights; the sole function of the state was simply the suppression of attempts by individuals to suppress other individuals, that is, to provide a secure and peaceful framework to facilitate social cooperation. While the means for determining who held the reins of government was to be decided democratically, the power and functions of government were significantly curtailed; the democracy of the classical liberal tradition was a strictly limited concept.

Before this ideal could be fully implemented, it began, like most ideals, to be abused. As suffrage was extended—which was not necessarily inimical in itself—this democracy became ever less limited. In exchange for votes, the politicians began to promise more and more. The function of the state, accordingly, could no longer be restricted to the protection of the life, liberty, and property of its citizens. The interventionist state thus began to supplant the laissez-faire state, even before the latter had been fully established. These statist measures were, in many cases, humanitarianly motivated, that is, aiding the poor, assistance for the jobless, and so on. Nevertheless, the inevitable corollary of this proliferation of government intervention was the precipitation of aggressive nationalism. It was the inevitable result of an ethos that sanctioned the extension of government into all phases of life. It was, in short, the emergence of the total state. Whether it came as autocracy or as the "despotism of the majority" was irrelevant.

Significance of National Boundaries

In a planned, autarkic economy, territorial boundaries are of supreme importance. An isolated nation must possess all of its required natural resources. The larger the area under control, the better it can provide for its wants and needs. Yet, no country is blessed with a position of complete economic self-sufficiency. Autarky, accordingly, must manifest itself in aggressive nationalism, in the desire of every country for the control of ever larger areas. What is required to make peace viable, therefore, is a lessening of the significance of boundaries.

This could only be attained, however, if the governments of the world were confined in their activities to protecting the life, liberty, and property of their citizens. Only then would international boundaries lose their significance. It would then make no difference whether a nation were large or small; its citizens could derive no benefit or sustain any damage from the extension or loss of territory. Under a laissez-faire system, where all transactions would take place between individuals unimpeded by government, the size of a nation would not matter. No one would be aided or hurt by a transfer of territorial jurisdiction, since all property would be held by individuals and all transactions would take place between individuals.

If the primacy of private property and free trade were the rule, at least one of the major causes of war would be all but eliminated. No one would be artifically or forcibly excluded, by tariff or immigration barriers, from acquiring any needed goods or natural resources. No one would be penalized for having been born a foreigner or of a different race or in a country of limited natural resources. Under these terms, then, at least one of the causes of war would be effectively ameliorated, if not eliminated entirely.

Conclusion

Statism, in so far as it begets autarky, engenders international antagonisms for which no peaceful solution can be found within the context of our contemporary politicio-economic ethos. These antagonisms can be relieved only by a change in ideologies. What is needed to make peace viable is the acceptance of the principles of limited democracy and its economic corollary, the free market. Only by such an advance can we ever hope to surmount at least one of the underlying factors precipitating international conflicts and war.

If this analysis possesses any cogency at all, then at least one thing is surely manifest: all the antiwar marches, protests, demonstrations, and peace songs from here to China cannot improve the situation one iota. While they may be fun, they are nevertheless futile. They are futile because they are premised upon a misunderstanding of war. Yet, wars continue to occur. Accordingly, war will not be ameliorated, much less abolished, by the mere utterance of platitudes or by shock tactics designed to scare us into peace. Only the elimination of its root cause can greatly diminish the threat of war. Such a policy, to repeat, entails a change in attitude, a policy impossible until the leaders and the people of the world are prepared to accept it.

1. As quoted by Edmund Opitz, *Religion and Capitalism* (New Rochelle: Arlington House, 1970), p. 268.
2. Easily the most lucid and cogent delineation of this position is to be found in Ludwig von Mises' *Omnipotent Government* (New Rochelle: Arlington House, 1969).

11

Welfare States at War

by Hans F. Sennholz

Perhaps the most startling thing about this essay by Hans F. Sennholz is that so little change would be required to bring it up-to-date. True, Nasser is referred to as the present dictator of Egypt, and his seizure of the Suez Canal is discussed as a recent event. But the words with which Dr. Sennholz begins: "The new international crises sparked in the Middle East, and the constant danger of another world war," still could refer to today's headlines, more than a generation after this article was published in the February 1957 Freeman. Dr. Sennholz takes as his main topic "how interventionist policies lead to economic nationalism," and provides real illustrations of ways in which we "hurt foreign producers in order to 'assist' our pressure groups" that are also still topical.

The seizure of the Suez Canal and its subsequent internationalization, with no thought of returning it to its owners, are used as examples of the muddling of moral issues in a protectionist world. Dr. Sennholz warns that we must reject "the principle that crime becomes righteousness if a previous crime remains unpunished." He offers instead some guidelines for a laissez-faire approach to international relations: support individual liberty and free enterprise, and don't assist or even diplomatically recognize protectionist governments.

The new international crises sparked in the Middle East, and the constant danger of another world war, need not surprise the student of contemporary international relations and economic policies. The ideology of socialism and interventionism has swayed our foreign relations, and the policies of Welfare States have destroyed international peace and order.

While throwing the blame for the present crises on the doorsteps of "capitalist colonialism," the Welfare States are battling each other. All parties involved in the Mideast are either socialist or interventionalist nations. Israel is a large army camp crowded by people who are given to socialist ideas; Egypt is an interventionist country with a dictator bent upon leading his nation to socialism;

France has a socialist government with controls that leave little room for competitive enterprise; and Britain is floundering between socialism and interventionism. In other words, there is little capitalism, in the sense of competitive private enterprise, in any one of these countries.

Absence of individual freedom and free enterprise makes for economic nationalism and international conflict. By fundamental nature and objective, the Welfare State controls private property and limits individual freedom in order to distribute economic spoils and privileges to pressure groups. The Welfare State is a favor state.

Pressure groups of producers expect the government to increase the prices of their products or services, with utter disregard for the economic interests of the vast majority of their own countrymen and of many foreign producers. In most cases of welfare legislation the favored group's foreign competition is either eliminated entirely or severely curtailed. This is economic nationalism, the most important source of international conflict.

Economic Nationalism Creates Conflict

Let us demonstrate how interventionist policies lead to economic nationalism with a few American examples. In order to enhance the price of sugar cane and beets produced by a few thousand American farmers, the federal government not only levies a highly protective sugar tariff, but also imposes severe import quotas. To afford our domestic producers a temporary gain, we partially close our markets to Central American sugar. In other words, we cause domestic prices of sugar to rise and depress foreign prices, subsidizing our sugar farmers at the expense of American consumers and Cuban farmers. This is economic nationalism.

Meanwhile, Soviet Russia takes political and economic advantage of our shortsighted "welfare policies." She buys Cuban sugar at depressed prices, thus appearing as benefactor to our southern neighbors.

In deference to our cattlemen, we prohibit the importation of cheap Argentine beef. That is to say, we favor domestic producers to the detriment of domestic consumers and South American producers. These and similar acts have earned us the hostility of our Central and South American neighbors. Russia, of course, ably utilizes our trade restrictions for her own purchase policies. Her efficient propaganda then interprets our behavior as capitalist imperialism, and her own as a token of communist friendship.

Similar acts of economic nationalism on the part of our federal government include the recent tariff increases on Swiss watches, the import restrictions on foreign dairy products, and many others. In each instance we severely hurt foreign producers in order to "assist" our pressure groups.

West Sets Bad Example

Of course, the other Western powers are guilty of similar policies of economic nationalism. The United States, Britain, and France embarked upon the welfare road to international conflict after Imperial Germany had shown the way. In the 1880's the German government imposed heavy social costs on the German economy. The logical outcome would have been a loss of sales to foreign competition, with German unemployment. To avoid these undesired effects, the government created cartels. Behind high walls of protective tariffs these organizations then charged monopoly prices on the domestic market and dumped excess supplies on foreign markets at low prices. This was economic nationalism at its source.

Germany has become the classical example of government omnipotence in economic matters. There is scarcely any restriction on trade that was not practiced and fully developed in Germany. The people in underdeveloped areas, unaware of the meaning of individual liberty and capitalism, have admired this seemingly omnipotent power of the German state and often have endeavored to imitate it.

Britain's economic nationalism dates back to World War I and especially to the Import Duties Act and Ottawa Agreements of 1932. The preferential principle that became the guiding principle of British political action gave "home producers first protection, Commonwealth producers second protection, and foreign producers none at all." Britain imposed substantial duties on most foreign foodstuffs and raw materials in order to grant trade preferences to Commonwealth producers. Consequently, foreign sales in Great Britain declined considerably.

The Churchill government during World War II imposed a multiplicity of restrictions from the armory of socialism. The Labor government then went on to nationalize the "means of exchange," the coal mines, the gas and electricity industries, the iron and steel industries. It vested in a Central Land Board all development rights in land. It did its utmost to eliminate rent, profit, and interest in order to employ the revenue for projects of "national development." In all these acts of seizure of private property, the Labor government showed no hesitancy because of foreign investments. It seized them along with those of its own nationals. All this meant economic harm to foreigners, who watched and learned the lesson in government omnipotence.

Underdeveloped Areas Follow Suit

Can it be surprising, therefore, that governments in underdeveloped areas of the world finally began to imitate the West's own policies? Can we blame them for feeling free to do what they please provided they enjoy the backing of their own popular majorities? Indeed, they may have learned from us to seize and nationalize private property and arbitrarily to tear up contracts, including their own charters.

Colonel Nasser is a thorough student of Western welfare statism and economic nationalism. He desired revenue for a program of "national development." Why should he not seize the Suez Canal Company, this private corporation on Egyptian soil? What does it matter that his government was paid in full for the use of a desert strip before the Canal was built? What of Egyptian signatures to international agreements? What if there were government charters and promises? He enjoys the backing of a popular majority. Does this not make him omnipotent? Does this not lift him above the restraints of moral and ethical laws of human relations?

Can the sovereign state of Egypt be bothered that the private property it seizes happens to be the life line of British Commonwealth trade and controls the flow of Mideastern oil? What does it matter that the well-being of all Europe must deteriorate through his nationalization of the Canal? What other sovereign state considered foreign interests in the realization of its statist objectives? Influenced by such ideas, Colonel Nasser embarked upon his tragic policies of economic nationalism and international conflict.

The next move then was up to those whose property had been seized. Among the victims, the governments of France and Great Britain decided to seize the Canal by force, pending an international conference to discuss the Canal's internationalization. No party involved wants to return the Canal to its lawful owners. Internationalization and control by several governments, however, merely means collectivism and economic nationalism on a supergovernmental basis.

What Course Freedom?

The defender of private property and competitive enterprise, observing such an insoluble conflict, is at a loss regarding the question of guilt. Is he to sympathize with the culprit who started the conflict in order to finance various "welfare policies"? Or is he to sympathize with the socialized victims who resort to force, which is evil, in order to alleviate the original evil?

In sharp contrast to the international conflict between socialist governments in this Mideastern affair is the peaceful coexistence of laissez-faire nations, which realize the ideals of personal freedom of choice, private ownership and control of property, and peaceful exchange in a competitive market. Under this concept, the sole function of government is the protection of its own people from domestic peacebreakers and from foreign aggressors. Such a government would wage war only to defend the lives and property of its own citizens. This means that it should not participate in foreign wars that grow out of economic nationalism. For such warfare only destroys and does not protect life and property.

While an individual peacebreaker can easily be punished and isolated in a penitentiary, a collectivist nation conducting policies of economic nationalism can be disciplined and subjugated only through a full-scale war and subsequent occupation of its territory. To discipline a nation that refuses to embrace the doctrines of freedom and free enterprise is an endless and hopeless task.

A citizen of a free country who goes abroad should know that he travels at his own risk. Crossing the border of his state and entering socialist or interventionist territory is to leave law and order behind. He risks transgressions by the foreign state upon his life, liberty, and property. A businessman who invests his funds in collectivist territory must consider the risks of expropriation, foreign exchange control, confiscatory taxation, and many other "welfare" measures. He is beyond the protection of his capitalist government. He is on his own.

The Principles of World Leadership

Despite curbs and checks on its power, and its inaction in a world of conflict, a government designed for freedom is a natural leader. The creative power of a free nation by far excels that of socialist or interventionist countries of similar size. And it is productive strength that lends the position of leadership to a country in a world that is always fighting or preparing to fight.

But true leadership that exerts potent influence toward world peace and prosperity springs from a far more important source than material and military might. True leadership grows out of impeccable behavior and moral conduct. A leading nation that lacks these prerequisites can guide the world only to more chaos and conflict.

Above all, such a nation must refrain from any act of economic nationalism. It must not harm any other nation through "welfare" policies of its own. It must adhere to its own design for freedom. To reprimand other nations for policies of economic nationalism while waging economic war upon its own neighbors would be hypocrisy and sanctimony.

Throughout most of the nineteenth century Great Britain was a true world leader. Her famous open-door policy treated Britishers and foreigners alike. The Empire was a vast free-trade area in which the government merely undertook to maintain peace, law, and order. Most civilized nations soon followed suit in removing their trade barriers and adopting the Empire standard of exchange, the gold standard. The British government indeed led the world during the most peaceful century of human history.

A leading nation must also reject the immoral principle that one act of economic nationalism by one government sanctions the nationalistic policies of all other governments. This is the principle that crime becomes righteousness if a previous crime has remained unpunished. But this very assumption underlies many prevailing notions concerning foreign affairs.

Things We Can Do

World leadership demands that we should openly judge world events and explain the fallacy of every act of economic nationalism. If a foreign government contemplates or embarks upon economic aggression through "welfare" legislation, we should call attention to the inevitable harm inflicted upon other nations. We need not intervene forcibly, for nations cannot be coerced to peaceful coexistence. Only a change in political and economic outlook can bring this about.

Naturally, we would sign no treaty with a government that has disregarded its own agreements and torn up its own charters. Nor would we assist any government that nationalizes private industries, for then we would be helping to promote collectivism and ultimate destruction. There could be no point in our extending diplomatic recognition to any government that indulges in economic nationalism.

Finally, world leadership requires that we constantly defend the principles of individual liberty and free enterprise. At every opportunity we should call out to the world that only competitive private enterprise can lead to peace and prosperity. We have a glorious history of individual freedom and safety of property—the absence of nationalization and confiscation by an omnipotent state. Our recent excursions toward the Welfare State endanger our record—and ourselves. But if we will correct that trend, then with pride we can demonstrate to the warring world that individual liberty is the only durable foundation for peace and prosperity.

If our way is freedom, then other nations on their disastrous roads may someday listen to reason and follow us as all civilized nations followed Great Britain during the nineteenth century. Law, order, and peace may then return once again to a battered world suffering from an absence of individual freedom and free enterprise.

12

Free Trade and Foreign Wars

by Samuel H. Husbands

Although the United States was founded on the principles of free trade and no "entangling alliances," to use Thomas Jefferson's words, the seeds of protectionism and military intervention were sown as early as 1789, with the passage of the Merchant Marine Act, protecting our ships by granting a tariff differential on goods shipped in American holds. Mr. Husbands is a Trustee and past Chairman of the Board of The Foundation for Economic Education as well as an officer of a national investment banking firm. This essay, based on an address he presented at a FEE board meeting on December 5, 1982, was published in the April 1983 issue of The Freeman. *After raising the historical question of how the U.S. came to sanction protectionism and foreign intervention, and the role that the Merchant Marine Act and the Barbary Wars played in our early history, Mr. Husbands goes on to examine the economic fallacies underlying protectionism, paying particular attention to the recent history of oil and gas controls and their relationship to Middle East policy. Finally, he suggests a policy of free trade and a volunteer army to insure the survival of the United States while lessening the possibility of military interventionism; he also calls for the repeal of all legal restrictions on citizens who wish personally to aid causes in other nations. But above all, he stresses, we must recognize the danger for war in "foolish economic theories." A policy of international free trade is the best hope for peace.*

I t is my purpose to show that though the principles of free trade and no entangling alliances on which the nation was founded were unique and sublime, we find that economic fallacy, misplaced patriotism, and political compromise have combined to undermine the legacy of those principles.

In his First Annual Address to Congress in 1790, George Washington said "Observe good faith and justice toward all nations. Cultivate peace and harmony with all . . . The nation which indulges toward another an habitual hatred or an habitual fondness is in some degree a slave. It is a slave to its animosity or to its affection, either of which is sufficient to lead it astray from its duty and its interest . . . it is our true policy to steer clear of permanent alliances with any portion of the foreign world.''

In his First Inaugural Address in 1801 Thomas Jefferson stated that among his essential principles of governing would be a policy of ''peace, commerce and honest friendship with all nations—entangling alliances with none.''

And so it was that the Founding Fathers understood that for free men to remain free they must remain strong in their defense but avoid meddling in other nations' affairs.

The test of that resolution to remain free of foreign wars was to confront Washington and Jefferson in the first years of the Republic. A combination of events, including legislation passed as the Merchant Marine Act of July 4, 1789 and the acts of a quartet of Barbary powers were leading the nation to its first experience in foreign intervention, the results of which were as ambiguous as any of the dozen or so adventures abroad that were to follow to this day.

The Merchant Marine

The 1789 Merchant Marine Act instituted tariffs for revenue purposes, but with a tariff differential of 10 per cent on any goods shipped in American holds. The effect in stimulating the growth of a distinctly American Merchant Marine was startling, for in 1789 the United States was carrying 17½ per cent of her imports and 30 per cent of her exports. Within six years these numbers had become 92 per cent and 88 per cent, and yearly tonnage under the American flag had grown from 123,893 tons to 529,471 tons.

To advocates of free trade, any reduction in tariffs is good, no tariffs better, but the outgrowth of this selective tariff disparity was the ''American'' merchant marine. The promotion and protection of its ships and men became a patriotic duty. Just one hundred years later, in 1881, William Graham Sumner considered the necessity of a national merchant marine, and wrote:

> If Americans owned no ships and sailed no ships, but hired the people of other countries to do their ocean transportation for them, it would simply prove that Americans had some better employment for their capital and labor. They would get transportation as cheaply as possible. That is all they care for, and it would be as foolish for any nation to insist on doing its own ocean transportation, devoting to this use capital and labor which might be otherwise more profitably employed, as it would be for a merchant to insist on doing his own carting, when some person engaged in carting offered him a contract on more advantageous terms than those on which he could do the work.

The seizure of American merchant ships and sailors in the late 18th century by

Barbary rulers, and to a lesser extent the harassment of American shipping by the picaroons of the West Indies, brought humiliation to the young nation. The resulting pressure on its political leaders led the country to embark on a program of rapid construction of six imposing frigates, the 44-gun "United States," "Constitution," and "President" along with the 33-gun "Constellation," "Chesapeake," and "Congress."

The construction of these first elements of the U.S. Navy found support from Northern ship-owning families, but only disinterest or even animosity from most Southerners, who were not as concerned about what flag flew over the ship that took their cotton to English and Continental mills.

The legitimate defense of the territory of the United States may have been a beneficiary of the emergence of the U.S. Navy, but the immediate stimulus to the construction of warships seems to have been the urgency to protect American civil shipping in far off corners of the world. The early adoption of a far-flung policing function for the U.S. government was a precedent which allowed later interventions abroad to come about with less controversy.

The Barbary Wars

The Barbary Wars were to last from 1800 to 1815, at a cost of hundreds of lives and millions of dollars for, at first, tribute and ransom, followed by the expense of construction of ships and naval operations in the Mediterranean. However, direct military intervention is only the most observable of the many ways in which we as a nation became "slaves to habitual hatred or fondness" for the people of other nations.

Were man perfectible the concept of nationhood might be obsolete. In the absence of that perfectibility, the nation state is likely to survive though I should hope as only a shadow of its present size. Man's institutions, like man himself, are imperfect, and must be vigilantly watched lest they assume unintended roles. When acts are made in the name of the state which are contemptuous of liberty and the good sense of market economics, and which may in fact lead toward war, they must be exposed for the menace they may present to the Republic.

Rhodes Boyson, Britain's Minister of Education, has likened man to a three-legged stool, one leg being moral or religious, one economic and one tribal. Dark deeds have been done in the name of each of these aspects of man's character, but in this century the tribal and economic elements have dominated man's actions, at least in the West. Economic fallacy teamed with rampant nationalism and without moral balance has proved to be a terribly costly affair in lives lost, economic deprivation and cultural undermining.

And so it is that military conflict stems not only from such obvious causes as pure territorial aggrandizement and gratification of monumental egos, but often from a military extension of economic fallacies. Economic nationalism is invariably a partner of military intervention.

Some of the fallacies and interventions that always accompany them, include notions of the necessity for:

(1) A favorable balance of trade.

(2) The protection of domestic industry.

A few of the interventions that logically proceed from these fallacies include protective tariffs, import quotas, domestic subsidies, antidumping laws, and currency controls.

Underlying all of these interventions is the notion that government through fiat actions can cause beneficial outcomes without offsetting costs. One does not have to be the complete cynic to suggest that what might be argued on the theoretical level in economic terms comes down in fact to a political formula: Can one group of voters be satisfied through a visible hand-out while another group of voters, affected adversely, and often unknowingly, by interventionist legislation, be mollified through dissembling and obfuscation?

One of the textbook excuses for tariffs has been that they were necessary to protect infant industry. Now that has been modified so that we are led to believe we must also protect mature, ailing industry. In fact, it is only with free trade that entrepreneurs are encouraged and noncompetitive enterprises are culled out, and these are two sides of a vigorous, productive and free economy.

There are then the laws which reinforce the notion that exports are better than imports, known as a "favorable" balance of trade. Bastiat, the 19th-century French economist, took the favorable balance of trade argument to its logical end, and suggested that were such a thing so desirable, the custom agents should record the export of French silks to Britain and hope the ships will founder, since the result would be a recording of, say, 1,000,000 francs as an export and no offsetting import, since the silk manufacturer has received no payment with which to purchase British goods. The result would be a favorable balance of trade, but we needn't envy France for having achieved that goal.

Balance of Payments and Balance of Trade

Balance of payments refers to the accounting between nations of all goods, services and financial transfers. On a pure gold standard or pure flexible exchange rate basis, balance of payments tend to balance on a regular basis. Balance of trade is this figure less "invisibles" or cash transfers.

Jacques Rueff demonstrated in his book *Balance of Payments* that France had an "unfavorable" balance of trade with Germany for over 50 years from 1870–1933, with the exception of the four years after the Franco-Prussian War, when France was making reparation payments to Germany. Again, the act which causes the "favorable" blance of trade is obviously not in the interest of French citizens at large, but may only favor certain special interests. The reason for the long period of French-Prussian balance of payments situation was, of course, the result of the dominant French investments in Germany.

This necessitated a French "unfavorable" balance of trade in order to offset intangibles such as dividends and interest accruing from French investments in Germany.

Milton Friedman has made the observation that the most favorable situation that could visit a people would be that in which we send dollar bills to Japan in exchange for automobiles, and the exchange ends there. If Japan were a willing partner to that transaction we could all retire. The absurdity is obvious.

Extending the Logic

What difference, in moral or economic terms, is there between a New Yorker buying an automobile built in California by a naturalized Japanese-American or an automobile built in Yokohama by a Japanese national? Yes, one is American and the other Japanese, but if that argument has merit why not extend it backward and suggest that no New Yorker buy anything not made in New York, or extend it even further, and suggest that it would be in the interest of the denizens of Manhattan to buy no item not made on the island. One thing, for sure, there wouldn't be much to eat, certainly no bananas.

Unfortunately, the Constitutional prohibitions against tariffs did not extend to international trade.

One often hears that free trade is fine, but not unfair trade, that being defined variously as everything from foreign government subsidy of exports to foreign workers receiving relatively lower wages. "Dumping," a useful pejorative, is generally considered the extreme variant of unfair trade. Dumping refers to goods being sold in this country at a price below which they are sold in the country of origin. I daresay the network news commentators would look with favor on an announcement by the British government that it was going to give away 10,000 Rolls Royces to a random group of lucky American citizens, in gratitude for American help in World War II.

It is highly unlikely that even the American automobile industry could rally much of a boycott against such an act, though it would remove those 10,000 individuals as potential customers for Detroit autos. There is no economic difference between such a daft proposal and that act of constructing and operating the Concorde supersonic aircraft, with losses made up each day by French and British taxpayers. Each traveler on the Concorde could consider the advantageous speed the aircraft offers as a partial gift by those taxpayers. However, the United States should have a difficult time working up much of a lather over foreign government subsidies for their businesses when we have such institutions as the Export-Import Bank, agricultural subsidies and Federal insurance on foreign investment.

Tariffs for Protection

U.S. tariffs were primarily a revenue-raising device prior to the Civil War. The first tariff passed in 1789 raised half of the nation's fiscal needs, and by 1808 duties were providing twice the federal government's expenditures. By 1816 tariffs were becoming specifically protective and by the 1970s when revenues from duties only totaled 10 per cent or so of the budget, their nature had evolved almost purely into protectionist devices.

Historically, Republicans have been defenders of high duties, Democrats lower duties. At the moment, sympathy for protectionist tariffs seems to be a bi-partisan affair. As mentioned earlier, protectionist tariffs have always been introduced on the ground that a particular industry is threatened by foreign competition. For the sake of jobs and the long-term future of the country, imports, under this persuasion, must be selectively restricted. What those advocates fail to point out is that for everyone who benefits from tariffs there are others, perhaps less observable, who are being economically punished.

The recently passed quotas on the importations of steel, at the behest of domestic steel management and labor leaders, have received nothing but plaudits by the favorably affected industries and the media, though often couched in terms such as "the act is too little or too late." One would have to seek out journals of economic opinion, and selective ones at that, to find mention of those who suffer as a consequence of those import quotas.

Currency restrictions and pegged exchange rates are put in place to cover up governmental overspending and inflation, and to exert control over citizens in their attempts to make voluntary transactions with others or to avoid government's confiscation of their accumulated wealth. It is a delaying tactic; no matter how severe the penalty, if the free market exchange ratio of two currencies is different from that dictated by government, the pegged price will be undermined by market forces resulting in sudden and catastrophic devaluation. U.S. laws to make it a felony to move more than $5,000 in or out of the country without reporting it only reinforce those who see it their business to run others' lives.

However, the most melancholy of all these false economic persuasions is autarky or National Economic Independence. What inevitably follows the embracing of this concept is the implied or real expansion of national borders with consequent recourse to military action. One of the major differences that divided Hitler and his finance minister, Hjalmar Schacht, was over this concept of economic independence. How unsettling when we have words from Wall Street to Washington that sound so familiarly like those of Hitler when he suggested the necessity for economic mobilization "comparable to the military and political mobilization."

The Pattern of Controls

Though the imposition of Wage and Price controls in 1971 was done in the name of controlling inflation, those controls remaining on oil and gas caused the government to begin to intervene in the classic manner of politicians anywhere who believe in the economic and political benefit of autarky.

The United States is widely regarded as the marginal factor in world production and consumption of oil. The steps that follow essentially led this country to place a *floor under* the price of oil not a *ceiling over* the price of oil as the Department of Energy bureaucracy would have led us to believe.

Step 1. 1971—Wage and Price controls instituted.

Step 2. Most controls removed in 1973 but kept on oil and gas.

Step 3. OPEC raises prices drastically.

Step 4. We counter, irrationally, with the "entitlements" scheme encouraging imports, and price controls, discouraging domestic production.

Step 5. We don the national hair shirt of a contrived energy crisis and directly intervene in the auto industry through mileage requirements and 55 m.p.h. speed limit.

Step 6. This forced draft downsizing causes extraordinary capital expenditures and dislocations in the American automobile industry.

Step 7. Japanese and German auto manufacturers find themselves in the fortuitous position of manufacturing automobiles that are now perfect for the American market, this having come about because of their own governments over the years imposing three times the taxes on gasoline as in the U.S.

Step 8. The U.S. government urging National Energy Independence through subsidy and tax break, resulting in unnecessary and uneconomic allocation of capital to "alternate" fuel sources.

Step 9. All of this resulting in a disabling of the domestic automobile and steel industries and immeasurable costs to all the Western world.

One frequently hears that our presence in the Middle East is necessary to protect "our" oil. The implication is that in our absence, the oil would necessarily fall into unfriendly hands and those parties would then embargo exports to the United States. Ironically, *Business Week* reports on November 8, 1982, that "Standard Oil of California and Texaco are reportedly trying to minimize their take of Saudi oil in favor of cheaper Russian and Mexican oil." In fact, another "lubricant," ball bearings, owes its existence to the importation of chromium ore. Ninety per cent of what is used in this country comes from abroad, the Soviet Union being one of the largest suppliers.

Does our dependence on importation of chromium or other exotic minerals require government's intervention to insure supplies? I would suggest quite the contrary, for it is the reliance on the market place and individual initiative which will insure our supplies. As Hans Landsberg, Senior Fellow at Resources for the Future, says in a *Forbes* article of November 22, 1982: "We preach belief in market forces but we abandon reliance on them too easily."

Intervention Policies at Home Lead to Conflict Abroad

Each step we take to insure National Economic Independence carries us ever closer to military conflict. Our Middle Eastern commitments have now grown to the point that troop strength assigned to the Rapid Deployment Force is 230,000 soldiers, sailors and marines, that number to double in coming months. Its assigned area of operations will cover 20 countries in the Middle East, excluding Israel. The force, it is reported, will take on responsibility with the objective of strengthening friendly nations *politically* and militarily. How far removed that notion is from those admonishments of George Washington at the founding of the Republic!

A logical step that follows the notion of economic independence is the use of sanctions and embargoes. It is with these acts that we skate close to the pitfall of war. The problem is that sanctions by definition inhibit the market and precipitate reactions from perceived or real enemies which may have been unnecessary in their absence.

Pinpointing the root cause of any war is precarious. A colleague noticed some graffiti in San Francisco around Columbus Day which said: "World War III started when Columbus took away the land from the Indians." Of course, using that logic, the apple would be at the core of all our problems. One can, nonetheless, wonder whether the oil and steel embargo of Japan and the resulting fall of the Konoye government in October, 1941 did not in turn lead to the controversial exchange of the Greater East Asia Co-Prosperity Sphere for Communist hegemony throughout a major part of the Far East. The resultant loss of lives made the earlier Rape of Nanking appear an almost minor tragedy of this tragic century.

Steps for Survival

But what steps should the United States take to insure its survival in what can be a most unfriendly world?

It first must insure its priorities are right from the perspective of its uniqueness as a liberty loving, free market, limited government example to the world. Free trade is an inherent part of that profile. The maintenance of the military necessary to defend the country from aggressive acts can only be consistent with the American ideal of choice if it is maintained by voluntary enlistment. One hears much about one's obligation to make a "fair share" contribution to causes.

There is a rule of thumb that in voluntary associations, 20% of the members contribute 80% of the time and money necessary to keep the effort going. Any notion that even with a draft there is an even sharing of responsibility for the defense of the country falls in the face of the evidence that few soldiers in any war are in line operations, and one study shows that fewer than 50% of those acutally fire at the enemy.

Ronald Reagan said in a letter to Senator Mark Hatfield on May 5, 1980 that "draft registration may actually decrease our military preparedness, by making people think we have solved our defense problems when we have not. . . . But perhaps the most fundamental objection to draft registration is moral. Only in the most severe national emergency does the government have the claim to the mandatory service of its young people. In any other time, a draft or draft registration destroys the very values that our society is committed to defend."

Milton Friedman in a debate with a U.S. general at Stanford University defended the pro-volunteer Army position. The General scoffed that he did not want to be defended by "an army of mercenaries." "Would you rather," Friedman replied, "be defended by an army of slaves?"

With the exception of President Reagan's implication that there might be emergencies in which the draft was desirable, I would otherwise agree with both in abhorrence of the use of force to conscript people to defend the country.

Defensible Action

The full-time job is the nourishment of the precepts of liberty at home and noninterference with other nations' affairs abroad. There will always be good men and women who will come to the defense of such an arrangement.

If foreign intervention tends to erode domestic liberty—as I would contend—there may still be instances where American citizens wish to put in with others they perceive to be suffering. The repeal of the legal inhibitions, including the Logan Act, preventing individuals from aiding those in other nations would expand free choice with no perceived risk to a nation bent on limiting its government's role.

Obviously, it is the understanding of and the willingness to stand by the principles of free choice which underlie the maintenance of a free society. What could be better than a rereading by veterans of free market theory or a first reading by a novice of Bastiat's works, or Henry Hazlitt's *Economics in One Lesson* or Leonard Read's "Conscience on the Battlefield" to make certain the argument on behalf of freedom remains articulate and principled?

Above all else it is vital that if the case for liberty is to prevail, the dangers of war posed by imposition of foolish economic theories be recognized and free exchange be applied to international as well as domestic trade. The saying is as true today as it was a century ago, "If goods do not cross borders, soldiers will."

Part Four

The Practice of Peace

This book has spent most of its pages on analyzing mistakes. What are the major fallacies that are summoned to promote protectionism, and how can they be refuted? How have protectionist policies in their various guises led to war, starvation, mass unemployment, and depression? How have seemingly humanitarian interventions in the economy produced a series of conflicts that makes the twentieth century the bloodiest century in the history of Western civilization?

Now it is time to turn to the positive. The last two essays in Part Three both anticipated this section in part, by sketching in how nations might protect their national interest by adopting free trade principles. Here we examine in more detail two positive suggestions for productive foreign relations. Gary North's essay addresses itself to a topic currently very much in the news as we go to press—"unfair trade practices." How should a nation respond when other countries subsidize goods for export or bar foreigners from certain protected markets? As the question has been raised in the U.S. Congress recently, it has been "Should we let them get away with it, or should we give them back tit for tat?" Gary North suggests a new kind of trade "war," one in which we drop trade barriers when barriers are raised against us, and he shows the kinds of unbelligerent victory and the benefits to which that policy could lead. Then Henry Hazlitt analyzes what we could gain from international investment as a substitute for foreign aid, giving us some unsettling figures about the relationship of aid to deficit spending in the process. Bettina Bien Greaves provides a summary overview of a foreign policy aimed at peace and prosperity, as a final chapter.

The epilogue, extracted from an article Frank Chodorov orignially wrote for the December 1950 issue of *analysis*, makes the simple point that the market-place is peaceful association, and any political intervention brings friction. In economic matters, we cannot have both peace and politics. And the act of trading is the practice of peace.

13

Tariff War, Libertarian Style
by Gary North

As this book is being compiled, polls show that a majority of the American public believes that the countries we trade with are unfair to us, and, as a result, that we are being victimized. It is widely complained that many other countries do not "play by the rules," but subsidize their exports and don't allow imports from us, thus hurting our economy. In this ingenious article, first published in 1969 in The Freeman, *Gary North analyzes the concept of the "tariff war" that has arisen from similar perceptions in the past. Since our ultimate economic goal is prosperity, he points out, the goals of our trade policy should be to make our exports attractive and to maintain the international division of labor. Therefore, rather than engage in the usual form of tariff war, which weakens the international division of labor by erecting higher and higher barriers to trade, our best retaliation to "unfair trade practices" would be to drop all trade barriers ourselves. Although details in this article may show its age—for example, it was written when it was still possible for foreign nations to demand that we convert dollars to gold—none of them cloud the cogency of the argument, which is as fresh as today's newspaper. Dr. North publishes two newsletters,* The Remnant Review *and* Biblical Economics Today, *and is President of the Institute for Christian Economics in Tyler, Texas.*

"Common sense economics" is a phrase used to describe the economic reasoning of the proverbial man in the street. In many instances, this knowledge may rest on principles that are essentially correct. For example, we have that old truism that there are no free lunches. If some of our professional experts in the field of governmental fiscal policy were to face the reality of this truth, they might learn that even the skilled application of policies of monetary inflation cannot alleviate the basic economic limitations placed on mankind.[1] Such policies can make things worse, of course, but they are powerless to do more than redistribute the products of industry, while simultaneously redistributing power in the direction of the state's bureaucratic functionaries.[2] On the other hand, not all of the widely-held economic beliefs are even remotely correct;

some of these convictions are held in inverse proportion to their validity. The tariff question is one of these.

The heart of the contradictory thinking concerning tariffs is in the statement, "I favor open competition, but. . . . " Being human, men will often appeal to the State to protect their monopolistic position on the market. They secretly favor security over freedom. The State steps in to honor the requests of certain special interest groups—which invariably proclaim their cause in the name of the general welfare clause of the Constitution—and establishes several kinds of restrictions on trade.

Fair trade laws are one example. They are remnants of the old medieval conception of the so-called "just price," in that both approaches are founded on the idea that there is some underlying objective value in all articles offered for sale. Selling price should not deviate from this "intrinsic" value.[3] Monopolistic trade union laws are analogous to the medieval guild system; they are based in turn upon restrictions on the free entry of nonunion laborers into the labor market.

Tariffs, trade union monopolies, and fair trade laws are all praised as being safeguards against "cutthroat" competition, i.e., competition that would enable consumers to purchase the goods they want at a cheaper price—a price which endangers the less efficient producers who must charge more in order to remain in business. The thing which most people tend to overlook in the slogan of "cutthroat competition" is that the person whose throat is slashed most deeply is the solitary consumer who has no monopolistic organization to improve his position in relation to those favored by Statist intervention.

People are remarkably schizophrenic in their attitudes toward competition. Monopolies of the supply of labor are acceptable to most Americans; business monopolies are somehow evil. In both cases, the monopolies are the product of the State in the market, but the public will not take a consistent position with regard to both. The fact that both kinds operate in order to improve the economic position of a limited special interest group at the expense of the consumers is ignored. Business monopolies are damned no matter what they do. If they raise prices, it is called *gouging*; if they cut prices, it is *cutthroat competition*; if they stabilize prices, it is clearly a case of collusion *restraining free competition*. All forms may be prosecuted. No firm is safe.

The State's policies of inflation tend to centralize production in the hands of those firms that are closest to the newly created money—defense industries, space-oriented industries, and those in heavy debt to the fractional reserve banking system. It is not surprising that we should witness a rising tide of corporate mergers during a period of heavy inflationary pressures, as has been the case during the 1960s in the United States. Yet, with regard to business firms (but not labor unions), the courts are able to take action against almost any firm which is successfully competing on the market.

As Dr. Richard Bernhard has pointed out, "What is becoming illegal under federal law in the United States is monopolizing—as the law now defines monopolizing; and, since this is now considered a crime, it is possible that perfectly legitimate business actions by one firm may, if they 'inadvertently' lead to monopoly power, put a firm in jeopardy of the law."[4] Thus, we see a rational economic response on the part of business firms—consolidation for the sake of efficiency on an increasingly inflationary market—prosecuted by the State which has created those very inflationary pressures. There is an inconsistency somewhere.

Tariffs Are Taxes

A tariff is a special kind of tax. It is a tax paid directly by importers for the right to offer foreign products for sale on a domestic market. Indirectly, however, the tax is borne by a whole host of people, and these people are seldom even aware that they are paying the tax.

First, let us consider those in the United States. One group affected adversely by a tariff is that made up of consumers who actually purchase some foreign product. They pay a higher price than would have been the case had no duty been imposed on the importer. Another consumer group is the one which buys an American product at a high price which is protected by the tariff. Were there no tariff, the domestic firms would either be forced to lower their prices or shift to some line of production in which they could compete successfully. Then there is the nonconsumer group which would have entered the market had the lower prices been in effect; their form of the "tax" is simply the inability to enjoy the use of products which might have been available to them had the State not intervened in international trade.

Others besides the consumers pay. The importer who might have been able to offer cheaper products, or more of the products, if there had been no tariff, is also hurt. His business is restricted, and he reaps fewer profits. All those connected with imports are harmed. Yet, so are exporters. They find that foreign governments tend to impose retaliatory tariffs on our products going abroad. Even if those governments do not, foreigners have fewer dollars to spend on our products, because we have purchased fewer of theirs.

Two groups are obviously aided. The inefficient domestic producer is the recipient of an indirect government subsidy, so he reaps at least short-run benefits. The other group is the State itself; it has increased its power, and it has increased its revenues. (It is conceivable to imagine a case where higher revenues might in the long run result from lower tariffs, since more volume would be involved, so we might better speak of short-run increases of revenue.) We could also speak of a psychological benefit provided for all those who erroneously believe that protective tariffs actually protect them, but this is a benefit based on ignorance, and I hesitate to count it as a positive effect.

A *second* consideration should be those who are hurt abroad, although we seldom look at those aspects of tariffs. Both foreign importers and exporters are hurt, for the same reasons. The fewer foreign goods we Americans buy, the fewer dollars they have to spend on American goods and services. This, in turn, damages the position of foreign consumers, who must restrict purchases of goods which they otherwise might afford. This leaves them at the mercy of their own less efficient producers, who will not face so much competition from the Americans, since the availability of foreign exchange (U.S. dollars) is more restricted.

The tariff, in short, penalizes the efficient on both sides of the border, and it subsidizes the inefficient. If we were to find a better way of providing "foreign aid" to other countries, we might provide them with our goods (which they want) by purchasing their goods (which we want). That would be a noninflationary type of aid which would benefit both sides, rather than our present system which encourages bullies in our government and creates resentment abroad.

Protecting Vital Industries

What about our vital industries, especially our wartime industries? If they are driven out of business by cheaper foreign goods, what will we do if we go to war and find our trading patterns disrupted? Where will we find the skilled craftsmen?

There is some validity to this question, but it is difficult to measure the validity in a direct fashion. It is true that certain skills, such as watchmaking, might be unavailable in the initial stages of a war. There are few apprentice programs available in the United States in some fields. Nevertheless, if there really is a need for such services, would it not be better to subsidize these talents directly? If we must impose some form of tax subsidy, is it not always preferable to have the costs fully visible, so that benefits might be calculated more efficiently?

A tariff is a tax, but few people ever grasp this fact. Thus, they are less willing to challenge the tax, re-examine it periodically, or at least see what it is costing. Indirect taxes are psychologically less painful, but the price paid for the anesthetic of invisibility is the inability of men to see how the State is growing at their expense. What Tocqueville referred to as the "Bland Leviathan"—a steadily, imperceptibly expanding State—thrives on invisible and indirect taxes like inflation, tariffs, and monthly withdrawals from paychecks.[5] It ought to be a basic libertarian position to discover alternative kinds of tax programs, in an effort to reduce the economic burden of the State by making the full extent of taxation more obvious.

Trade War, Statist Style

One advantage of the direct subsidy to protected industries is that such subsidies would not normally result in trade wars. When one nation sees its products discriminated against by another State, it is more apt to retaliate directly. It threatens to raise tariffs against the offending country's products unless the first country's tariffs are reduced. If there is no response, pressures arise within the threatening country's State bureaus to enforce the threat. That, it is argued, will frighten other nations which might be considering similar moves. So the tariff war is born. The beneficiaries are the inefficient on both sides of the border and the State bureaucrats; the losers are all those involved in trade and all consumers who would have liked to purchase their goods at lower prices. This kind of war is therefore especially pernicious: it penalizes the productive and subsidizes the unproductive.

There are many reasons why these wars get started. During periods of inflation, certain countries wish to keep their domestic currencies from going abroad. These currencies, if they have international acceptability, are grounded in gold or in reserve currencies theoretically redeemable in gold. Foreign central banks can ask for repayment, and the inflating nations can be put into extreme financial embarrassment when too many of these claims are presented at one time. So they try to restrict purchases of foreign goods by their domestic populations. Tariffs are one way of accomplishing this end. Tariffs, in short, prevent international "bank runs," at least for limited periods of time.

Another cause is the fear of State bureaucrats during times of recession or depression that domestic industries will not be favored when domestic populations buy from abroad. This was the case under the infant neomercantile philosophies so popular in the 1930s.[6] The depression was accompanied by a wave of tariff hikes in most of the Western nations, with reduced efficiency and economic autarky as a direct result. Domestic manufacturers cry for protection from foreign producers. What they are crying for with equal intensity is protection from the voluntary decisions of their own nation's domestic purchasers; it takes two parties to make a trade, and protection from one is equally protection from the other.

The effect of tariff wars is reduced efficiency through a restriction of international trade. Adam Smith, in the opening pages of *Wealth of Nations*, presents his now famous argument that the division of labor is limited by the size of the market. Reduce the size of the market, and you reduce the extent of the division of labor. The cry for protection should be seen for what it is: a cry for a reduction in efficiency.

In a country like the United States, where less than 5 per cent of our national income stems from foreign trade, the cry is especially ludicrous. We hurt the other nations, whose proportion of international trade to national income is much higher (West Germany, Japan), without really aiding very many of our own producers. But there are so few vocal interest groups representing those who benefit from freer trade, while those who have a stake in the intervention of the State make certain that their lobbyists are heard in Washington. The scapegoat of "unfair foreign competition" may be small, but being small, it is at least easy to sacrifice.

The Balance of Trade

In precapitalistic days, economists believed that nations could experience permanent "favorable" balances of trade. A favorable balance was defined as one where you sold more goods abroad than you imported, thus adding to the national gold stock. Wealth was defined primarily in terms of gold (a position which, even if fallacious, makes more sense than the contemporary inclination to define wealth in terms of indebtedness). Prior to the publication of *Wealth of Nations* (1776), the philosopher, David Hume, disposed of the mercantilist errors concerning the balance of trade. His essays helped to convert Adam Smith to the philosophy of classical liberalism. Hume's essay, "Of the Balance of Trade," was published in 1752 in his *Political Discourses*; it established him as a founder of modern international trade theory.

The early arguments for free trade still stand today. Hume focused on the first one, which is designated in modern economic terminology as the *price rate effect*. As the exported goods flow out of a nation, specie flows in. Goods become more scarce as money becomes more plentiful. Prices therefore tend to rise. The converse takes place in the foreign country: its specie goes out as goods come in, thus causing prices to fall. Foreign buyers will then begin to reduce their imports in order to buy on the now cheaper home markets; simultaneously, consumers in the first nation will now begin to export specie and import foreign goods. A long-run equilibrium of trade is the result.

A second argument is possible, the *income effect*. Export industries profit during the years of heavy exports. This sector of the economy is now in a position to effect domestic production, as its share of national income rises. It will be able to outbid even those foreign purchasers which it had previously supplied with goods.

Last, we have the *exchange rate effect*. If we can imagine a world trading community in which we have free floating exchange rates on the international currency markets (which most governments hesitate to permit), we can see the process more easily. In order to purchase domestic goods, foreigners must have a supply of the exporting nation's domestic currency. As demand for the goods continues, the supply of available currency drops lower. Foreigners competitively bid up the price of the exporting nation's currency, so that it costs more to obtain the currency necessary to buy the goods. This will discourage some of the foreign buyers, who will turn to their own markets. Where we find fixed exchange rates, the same process exists, but under different circumstances. Either black markets in foreign currencies will be established, or else some kind of quota restrictions will be placed on the availability of the sought-after currency, as demand rises for exchange. Foreigners will simply not be able to obtain all the currency they want at the official price. Thus, what we witness is an equilibriating process of the exchange of goods; there can be no long-run imbalance of trade. No nation can continue to export more than it imports forever.[7]

Tariff War, Libertarian Style

When some foreign State decides to place restrictions on the importation of goods from another country, what should be the response of that latter country's economic administrators? Their goal is to make their nation's goods attractive to foreign purchasers. They should want to see the international division of labor maintained, adding to the material prosperity of all involved. If this is the goal, then policies that will keep the trade barriers at low levels should be adopted. Instead, there is the tendency to adopt retaliatory tariff barriers, thus stifling even further the flow of goods. This is done as a "warning" to other nations.

If the 1930s are anything like representative years of such warnings, then we should beware of conventional tariff wars. In those years a snowballing effect was produced, as each nation tried to "out-warn" its neighbor in an attempt to gain favorable trade positions with all others. The result was the serious weakening of the international specialization of labor and its productivity. At a time when people wanted cheaper goods, they imposed trade restrictions which forced prices upward and production downward. Professor Mises' old dictum held true: When a State tries to improve economic conditions by tampering with the free market, it usually succeeds in accomplishing precisely the results which it sought to avoid (or *officially* sought to avoid, at any rate).

The best policy for "retaliation" would be to *drop* all tariff barriers in response. A number of things would result from such action. For one thing, it would encourage the importation of the goods produced by the offending country. Then the three effects described earlier would go into operation. The offending nation would find that its domestic price level would rise, and that its citizens would be in a position to buy more foreign goods (including the goods of the discriminated country). What would be done with the currency or credits in the hands of citizens of the high tariff nation? They could not spend it at home. If we, as the injured party, continued to make it easy for our citizens to buy their goods, we would provide them with lots of paper money which could be most easily used to buy our goods in return. We would gain the use of the consumer goods produced abroad, and we would be losing only money. We would be getting the best possible goods for our money, so the consumer cannot complain; if we had imposed retaliatory tariffs, consumers would have had to settle for domestically produced goods of a less desirable nature (since the voluntary consumption patterns are restricted by the imposition of a tariff). Our prices would tend to go down, making our goods more competitive on the international markets.

The tariff is a self-defeating device. As American dollars came into the high tariff nation, they could be exchanged for our gold. But this would tend to increase the rate of inflation in that country, as the gold reserves would most likely serve as the foundation for an expansion of the domestic money supply. Domestic prices would climb, and the citizens would attempt to circumvent the tariffs in various ways. Black markets in foreign currencies and goods are established; foreign goods are purchased in spite of tariff barriers; pressures for freer trade can arise, especially if the discriminated nation has wisely refused to turn to retaliation in the traditional way.

The statist tariff war is irrational. It argues that because one's citizens are injured by one restriction on foreign trade, they can be aided by further restrictions on foreign trade. It is a contemporary manifestation of the old cliché, "He cut off his nose to spite his face." It is time that we accept the implications of David Hume's two-hundred-year-old arguments. The best way to overcome restrictions on trade, it would seem, is to establish policies that encourage people to trade more.

1. *Cf.* Gary North, *Marx's Religion of Revolution* (Nutley, New Jersey: Craig Press, 1968), pp. 56–57.

2. Bertrand de Jouvenel, *The Ethics of Redistribution* (New York: Cambridge University Press, 1951), pp. 72–73.

3. Gary North, "The Fallacy of 'Intrinsic Value'," *The Freeman* (June, 1969).

4. Richard C. Bernhart, "English Law and American Law on Monopolies and Restraints of Trade," *The Journal of Law and Economics* (1960), p. 142.

5. Robert Schuettinger, "Tocqueville and the Bland Leviathan," *The Freeman* (January, 1962).

6. The interests which, in times of prosperity, find it hard to enlist support for their conspiracies to rob the public of the advantages of cheapness and the division of labor, find a much more sympathetic hearing." Lionel Robbins, *The Great Depression* (London: Macmillan, 1934), p. 65.

7. Wilhelm Röpke, *International Economic Disintegration* (London: Hodge, 1942), ch. 3.

14

Foreign Investment
vs.
Foreign Aid

by Henry Hazlitt

This book would not be complete without a contribution from Henry Hazlitt, the author of the famous Economics in One Lesson *(among many other books) and a trustee of The Foundation for Economic Education since its founding in 1946. In this essay, which is from the October 1970 issue of* The Freeman, *he gives a detailed explanation of the case for foreign investment as perhaps the most valuable export or import the United States can have. By importing capital, he points out, backward countries can skip centuries of painstaking development; by exporting capital, nations as well as individual investors prosper. Paradoxically, although both parties to foreign investment are better off (as is the case with all trade), it is looked on with suspicion by both nations involved. On the other hand, foreign aid is popular. There has been increasing pressure in the United States since World War II not to invest but to give capital away in government-to-government aid—which not only distorts both economies involved, but costs billions in taxpayer dollars. These expensive foreign aid programs, Mr. Hazlitt reports, were sufficient to account for the total of the federal deficit in the 1946–70 period, and also sufficient to account for the balance-of-payment deficits of the same period. This last fact is particularly ironic because the government has blamed the balance-of-payment deficit on foreign investment, instead.*

Hazlitt concludes that stopping foreign aid and allowing unlimited foreign investment would truly help the poorer countries become productive, self-reliant, and more prosperous. Our present policy ''prolongs the poverty it is designed to cure.''

A t the beginning of Chapter III of his *History of England*, Thomas Babington Macaulay wrote:

"In every experimental science there is a tendency toward perfection. In every human being there is a wish to ameliorate his own condition. These two principles have often sufficed, even when counteracted by great public calamities and by bad institutions, to carry civilization rapidly forward. No ordinary misfortune, no ordinary misgovernment, will do so much to make a nation wretched as the constant effort of every man to better himself will do to make a nation prosperous. It has often been found that profuse expenditures, heavy taxation, absurd commercial restrictions, corrupt tribunals, disastrous wars, seditions, persecutions, conflagrations, inundations, have not been able to destroy capital so fast as the exertions of private citizens have been able to create it. It can easily be proved that, in our own land, the national wealth has, during at least six centuries, been almost uninterruptedly increasing. . . . This progress, having continued during many ages, became at length, about the middle of the eighteenth century, portentously rapid, and has proceeded, during the nineteenth, with accelerated velocity."

We too often forget this basic truth. Would-be humanitarians speak constantly today of "the vicious circle of poverty." Poverty, they tell us, produces malnutrition and disease, which produce apathy and idleness, which perpetuate poverty; and no progress is possible without help from outside. This theory is today propounded unceasingly, as if it were axiomatic. Yet the history of nations and individuals shows it to be false.

It is not only "the natural effort which every man is continually making to better his own condition" (as Adam Smith put it even before Macaulay) that we need to consider, but the constant effort of most families to give their children a "better start" than they enjoyed themselves. The poorest people under the most primitive conditions work first of all for food, then for clothing and shelter. Once they have provided a rudimentary shelter, more of their energies are released for increasing the quantity or improving the quality of their food and clothing and shelter. And for providing tools. Once they have acquired a few tools, part of their time and energies can be released for making more and better tools. And so, as Macaulay emphasized, economic progress can become accelerative.

One reason it took so many centuries before this acceleration actually began, is that as men increased their production of the means of subsistence, more of their children survived. This meant that their increased production was in fact mainly used to support an increasing population. Aggregate production, population, and consumption all increased; but per capita production and consumption barely increased at all. Not until the Industrial Revolution began in the late eighteenth century did the rate of production begin to increase by so much that, in spite of leading to an unprecedented increase in population, it led also to an increase in per capita production. In the Western world this increase has continued ever since. So a country can, in fact, starting from the most primitive conditions, lift itself from poverty to abundance. If this were not so, the world could never have arrived at its present state of wealth. Every country started poor. As a matter of historic fact, most nations raised themselves from "hopeless" poverty to at least a less wretched poverty purely by their own efforts.

Specialization and Trade

One of the ways by which each nation or region did this was by division of labor within its own territory and by the mutual exchange of services and products. Each man enormously increased his output by eventually specializing in a single activity—by becoming a farmer, butcher, baker, mason, bricklayer, or tailor—and exchanging his product with his neighbors. In time this process extended beyond national boundaries, enabling each nation to specialize more than before in the products or services that it was able to supply more plentifully or cheaply than others, and by exchange and trade to supply itself with goods and services from others more plentifully or cheaply than it could supply them for itself.

But this was only one way in which foreign trade accelerated the mutual enrichment of nations. In addition to being able to supply itself with more goods and cheaper goods as a result of foreign trade, each nation supplied itself with goods and services that it could otherwise not produce at all, and of which it would perhaps not even have known the existence.

Thus foreign trade *educates* each nation that participates in it, and not only through such obvious means as the exchange of books and periodicals. This educational effect is particularly important when hitherto backward countries open their doors to industrially advanced countries. One of the most dramatic examples of this occurred in 1854, when Commodore Perry at the head of a U.S. naval force "persuaded" the Japanese, after 250 years of isolation, to open their doors to trade and communication with the U.S. and the rest of the world. Part of Perry's success, significantly, was the result of bringing and showing the Japanese such things as a modern telescope, a model telegraph, and a model railway, which delighted and amazed them.

Some Steps May be Skipped

Western reformers today, praising some hitherto backward country, in Africa or Asia, will explain how much smarter its natives are than we of the West because they have "leaped in a single decade from the seventeenth into the twentieth century." But the leap, while praiseworthy, is not so surprising when one recalls that what the natives mainly did was to import the machines, instruments, technology, and know-how that had been developed during those three centuries by the scientists and technicians of the West. The backward countries were able to bypass home coal furnaces, gaslight, the street car, and even, in most cases, the railroad, and to import Western automobiles, Western knowledge of road-building, Western airplanes and airliners, telephones, central oil heaters, electric light, radio and television, refrigerators and air-conditioning, electric heaters, stoves, dishwashers and clothes washers, machine tools, factories, plants, and Western technicians, and then to send some of their youth to Western colleges and universities to become technicians, engineers, and scientists. The backward countries imported, in brief, their "great leap forward."

In fact, not merely the recently backward countries of Asia and Africa, but every great industrialized Western nation, not excluding the United States, owes a very great part—indeed, the major part—of its present technical knowledge and productivity to discoveries, inventions, and improvements imported from other nations. Notwithstanding the elegant elucidations by the classical economists, very few of us today appreciate all that the world and each nation owes to foreign trade, not only in services and products, but even more in knowledge, ideas, and ideals.

International Investment

Historically, international trade gradually led to international investment. Among independent nations, international investment developed inevitably when the exporters of one nation, in order to increase their sales, sold on short-term credit, and later on longer-term credit, to the importers of another. It developed also because capital was scarcer in the less developed nation, and interest rates were higher. It developed on a larger scale when men emigrated from one country to another, starting businesses in the new country, taking their capital as well as their skills with them.

In fact, what is now known as "portfolio" investment—the purchase by the nationals of one country of the stocks or bonds of the companies of another—has usually been less important quantitatively than this "direct" investment. In 1967 U.S. private investments abroad were estimated to total $93 billion, of which $12 billion were short-term assets and claims, and $81 billion long-term. Of American long-term private investments abroad, $22 billion were portfolio investments and $59 billion direct investments.

The export of private capital for private investment has on the whole been extremely profitable for the capital-exporting countries. In every one of the twenty years from 1945 to 1964 inclusive, for example, the income from old direct foreign investments by U.S. companies exceeded the outflow of new direct investments. In that twenty-year period new outflows of direct investments totaled $22.8 billion, but income from old direct investments came to $37.1 billion, plus $4.6 billion from royalties and fees, leaving an excess inflow of $18.9 billion. In fact, with the exception of 1928, 1929, and 1931, U.S. income from direct foreign investments exceeded new capital outlays in every year since 1919.[1]

Our direct foreign investments also greatly stimulated our merchandise exports. The U.S. Department of Commerce found that in 1964, for example, $6.3 billion, or 25 per cent of our total exports in that year, went to affiliates of American companies overseas.

It is one of the ironies of our time, however, that the U.S. government decided to put the entire blame for the recent "balance-of-payments deficit" on American investments abroad; and beginning in mid-1963, started to penalize and restrict such investment.

The advantages of international investment to the capital importing country should be even more obvious. In any backward country there are almost unlimited potential ventures, or "investment opportunities," that are not undertaken chiefly because the capital to start them does not exist. It is the domestic lack of capital that makes it so difficult for the "underdeveloped" country to climb out of its wretched condition. Outside capital can enormously accelerate its rate of improvement.

Investment from abroad, like domestic investment, can be of two kinds: the first is in the form of fixed interest-bearing loans, the second in the form of direct equity investment in which the foreign investor takes both the risks and the profits. The politicians of the capital-importing country usually prefer the first. They see their nationals, say, making 15 or 30 per cent annual gross profit on a venture, paying off the foreign lender at a rate of only 6 per cent, and keeping the difference as net profit. If the foreign investor makes a similar assessment of the situation, however, he naturally prefers to make the direct equity investment himself.

But the foreigner's preference in this regard does not necessarily mean that the capital-importing country is injured. It is to its own advantage if its government puts no vexatious restrictions on the form or conditions of the private foreign investment. For if the foreign investor imports, in addition to his capital, his own (usually) superior management, experience, and technical know-how, his enterprise may be more likely to succeed. He cannot help but give employment to labor in the capital-importing country, even if he is allowed to bring in labor freely from his own. Self-interest and wage-rate differentials will probably soon lead him to displace most of whatever common or even skilled labor he originally brings in from his own country with the labor of the host country. He will usually supply the capital-importing country itself with some article or amenity it did not have before. He will raise the average marginal productivity of labor in the country in which he has built his plant or made his investment, and his enterprise will tend to raise wages there. And if his investment proves particularly profitable, he will probably keep reinvesting most of his profits in it as long as the market seems to justify the reinvestment.

There is still another benefit to the capital-importing country from private foreign investment. The foreign investors will naturally seek out first the most profitable investment opportunities. If they choose wisely, these will also be the investments that produce the greatest surplus of market value over costs and are therefore economically most productive. When the originally most productive investment opportunities have been exploited to a point where the comparative rate of return begins to diminish, the foreign investors will look for the next most productive investment opportunities, originally passed over. And so on. Private foreign investment will therefore tend to promote the most rapid rate of economic improvements.

Foreigners Are Suspect

It is unfortunate, however, that just as the government of the private-capital-exporting country today tends to regard its capital exports with alarm as a threat to its "balance of payments," the government of the private-capital-importing country today tends to regard its capital imports at least with suspicion if not with even greater alarm. Doesn't the private-capital-exporting country make a profit on this capital? And if so, mustn't this profit necessarily be at the expense of the capital-importing country? Mustn't the latter country somehow be giving away its patrimony? It seems impossible for the anticapitalist mentality (which prevails among the politicians of the world, particularly in the underdeveloped countries) to recognize that both sides normally benefit from any voluntary economic transaction, whether a purchase-sale or a loan-investment, domestic or international.

Chief among the many fears of the politicians of the capital-importing country is that foreign investors "take the money out of the country." To the extent that this is true, it is true also of domestic investment. If a home owner in Philadelphia gets a mortgage from an investor in New York, he may point out that his interest and amortization payments are going out of Philadelphia and even out of Pennsylvania. But he can do this with a straight face only by forgetting that he originally borrowed the money from the New York lender either because he could not raise it at all in his home city or because he got better terms than he could get in his home city. If the New Yorker makes an equity investment in Pennsylvania, he may take out all the net profits; but he probably employs Pennsylvania labor to build his factory and operate it. And he probably pays out $85 to $90 annually for labor, supplies, rent, etc., mainly in Pennsylvania, for every $10 he takes back to New York. (In 1969, American manufacturing corporations showed a net profit after taxes of only 5.4 per cent on total value of sales.) "They take the money out of the country" is an objection against foreign investors resulting even more from xenophobia than from anticapitalism.

Fear of Foreign Control

Another objection to foreign investment by politicians of the capital-importing country is that the foreign investors may "dominate" the borrowing country's economy. The implication (made in 1965 by the de Gaulle government of France, for example) is that American-owned companies might come to have too much to say about the economic decisions of the government of the countries in which they are located. The real danger, however, is the other way round. The foreign-owned company puts itself at the mercy of the government of the host country. Its capital in the form of buildings, equipment, drilled wells and refineries, developed mines, and even bank deposits, may be trapped. In the last twenty-five years, particularly in Latin America and the Middle East, as American oil companies and others have found to their sorrow, the dangers of discriminatory labor legislation, onerous taxation, harassment, or even expropriation, are very real.

Yet the anticapitalistic, xenophobic, and other prejudices against private foreign investment have been so widespread, in both the countries that would gain from importing capital and the countries that would profit from exporting it, that the governments in both sets of countries have imposed taxes, laws and regulations, red tape, and other obstacles to discourage it.

At the same time, paradoxically, there has grown up in the last quarter-century powerful political pressures in both sets of countries in favor of the richer countries *giving capital away* to the poorer in the form of government-to-government "aid."

The Marshall Plan

This present curious giveaway mania (it can only be called that on the part of the countries making the grants) got started as the result of an historical accident. During World War II, the United States had been pouring supplies—munitions, industrial equipment, foodstuffs—into the countries of its allies and cobelligerents. These were all nominally "loans." American Lend-Lease to Great Britain, for example, came to some $30 billion and to Soviet Russia to $11 billion.

But when the war ended, Americans were informed not only that the Lend-Lease recipients could not repay and had no intention of repaying, but that the countries receiving these loans in wartime had become dependent upon them and were still in desperate straits, and that further credits were necessary to stave off disaster.

This was the origin of the Marshall Plan.

On June 5, 1947, General George C. Marshall, then American Secretary of State, made at Harvard the world's most expensive commencement address, in which he said:

"The truth of the matter is that Europe's requirements, for the next three or four years, of foreign food and other essential products—principally from America—are so much greater than her present ability to pay that she must have substantial additional help, or face economic, social, and political deterioration of a very grave character."

Whereupon Congress authorized the spending in the following three-and-a-half years of some $12 billion in aid.

This aid was widely credited with restoring economic health to "free" Europe and halting the march of communism in the recipient countries. It is true that Europe did finally recover from the ravages of World War II—as it had recovered from the ravages of World War I. And it is true that, apart from Yugoslavia, the countries not occupied by Soviet Russia did not go communist. But whether the Marshall Plan accelerated or retarded this recovery, or substantially affected the extent of communist penetration in Europe, can never be proved. What can be said is that the plight of Europe in 1947 was at least as much the result of misguided European governmental economic policies as of physical devastation caused by the war. Europe's recovery was far slower than it could have been, with or without the Marshall Plan.

This was dramatically demonstrated in West Germany in 1948, when the actions between June 20 and July 8 of Economic Minister Ludwig Erhard in simultaneously halting inflation, introducing a thoroughgoing currency reform, and removing the strangling network of price controls, brought the German "miracle" of recovery.

As Dr. Erhard himself described his action: "We decided upon and re-introduced the old rules of a free economy, the rules of *laissez-faire*. We abolished practically all controls over allocation, prices, and wages, and replaced them with a price mechanism controlled predominantly by money."

The result was that German industrial production in the second half of 1948 rose from 45 per cent to nearly 75 per cent of the 1936 level, while steel production doubled that year.

It is sometimes claimed that it was Germany's share of Marshall aid that brought on the recovery. But nothing similar occurred in Great Britain, for example, which received more than twice as much Marshall aid. The German per capita gross national product, measured in constant prices, increased 64 per cent between 1950 and 1958, whereas the per capita increase in Great Britain, similarly measured, rose only 15 per cent.

Once American politicians got the idea that the American taxpayer owed other countries a living, it followed logically that his duty could not be limited to just a few. Surely that duty was to see that poverty was abolished everywhere in the world. And so in his Inaugural Address of January 20, 1949, President Truman called for "a bold new program" to make "the benefits of our scientific advances and industrial progress available for the improvement and growth of underdeveloped areas. . . . This program can greatly increase the industrial activity in other nations and can raise substantially their standards of living."

Because it was so labeled in the Truman address, this program became known as "Point Four." Under it the "emergency" foreign aid of the Marshall Plan, which was originally to run for three or four years at most, was universalized, and has now been running for more than twenty years. So far as its advocates and built-in bureaucracy are concerned, it is to last until foreign poverty has been abolished from the face of the earth, or until the per capita "gap" between incomes in the backward countries and the advanced countries has been closed— even if that takes forever.

The cost of the program already is appalling. Total disbursements to foreign nations, in the fiscal years 1946 through 1970, came to $131 billion. The total net interest paid on what the U.S. borrowed to give away these funds amounted in the same period to $68 billion, bringing the grand total through the 25-year period to $199 billion.[2]

This money went altogether to some 130 nations. Even in the fiscal year 1970, the aid program was still operating in 99 nations and five territories of the world, with 51,000 persons on the payroll, including U.S. and foreign personnel. Congressman Otto E. Passman, chairman of the Foreign Operations Subcommittee on Appropriations, declared on July 1, 1969: "Of the three-and-a-half billion people of the world, all but 36 million have received aid from the U.S."

Domestic Repercussions

Even the colossal totals just cited do not measure the total loss that the foreign giveaway program has imposed on the American economy. Foreign aid has had the most serious economic side-effects. It has led to grave distortions in our economy. It has undermined our currency, and contributed toward driving us off the gold standard. It has accelerated our inflation. It was sufficient in itself to account for the total of our Federal deficits in the 1946–70 period. The $199 billion foreign aid total exceeds by $116 billion even the $83 billion increase in our gross national debt during the same years. Foreign aid has also been sufficient in itself to account for all our balance-of-payments deficits (which our government's policies blame on private foreign investment).

The advocates of foreign aid may choose to argue that though our chronic Federal budget deficits in the last 25 years *could* be imputed to foreign aid, we could alternatively impute those deficits to other expenditures, and assume that the foreign aid was paid for entirely by raising additional taxes. But such an assumption would hardly improve the case for foreign aid. It would mean that taxes during this quarter-century averaged at least $5 billion higher each year than they would have otherwise. It would be difficult to exaggerate the setbacks to personal working incentives, to new ventures, to profits, to capital investment, to employment, to wages, to living standards, that an annual burden of $5 billion in additional taxation can cause.

If, finally, we make the "neutral" assumption that our $131 or $199 billion in foreign aid (whichever way we choose to calculate the sum) was financed in exact proportion to our actual deficit and tax totals in the 25-year period, we merely make it responsible for part of both sets of evils.

In sum, the foreign aid program has immensely set back our own potential capital development. It ought to be obvious that a foreign giveaway program can raise the standards of living of the so-called "underdeveloped areas" of the world only by lowering our own living standards compared with what they could otherwise be. If our taxpayers are forced to contribute millions of dollars for hydroelectric plants in Africa or Asia, they obviously have that much less for productive investment in the U.S. If they contribute $10 million dollars for a housing project in Uruguay, they have just that much less for their own housing, or any other cost equivalent, at home. Even our own socialist and statist do-gooders would be shaken if it occurred to them to consider how much might have been done with the $131 or $199 billion of foreign aid to mitigate pollution at home, build subsidized housing, and relieve "the plight of our cities." Free enterprisers, of course, will lament the foreign giveaway on the far more realistic calculation of how enormously the production, and the wealth and welfare of every class of our population, could have been increased by $131 to $199 billion in more private investment in new and better tools and cost-reducing equipment, and in higher living standards, and in more and better homes, hospitals, schools, and universities.

The Political Arguments

What have been the economic or political compensations to the United States for the staggering cost of its foreign aid program? Most of them have been illusory.

When our successive Presidents and foreign aid officials make inspirational speeches in favor of foreign aid, they dwell chiefly on its alleged humanitarian virtues, on the need for American generosity and compassion, on our duty to relieve the suffering and share the burdens of all mankind. But when they are trying to get the necessary appropriations out of Congress, they recognize the advisability of additional arguments. So they appeal to the American taxpayer's material self-interest. It will redound to his benefit, they argue, in three ways:

1. It will increase our foreign trade, and consequently the profits from it. 2. It will keep the underdeveloped countries from going communist. 3. It will turn the recipients of our grants into our eternally grateful friends.

The answers to these arguments are clear:

1. Particular exporters may profit on net balance from the foreign aid program, but they necessarily do so at the expense of the American taxpayer. It makes little difference in the end whether we give other countries the dollars to pay for our goods, or whether we directly give them the goods. We cannot grow rich by giving our goods or our dollars away. We can only grow poorer. (I would be ashamed of stating this truism if our foreign aid advocates did not so systematically ignore it.)

2. There is no convincing evidence that our foreign aid played any role whatever in reversing, halting, or even slowing down any drift toward communism. Our aid to Cuba in the early years of the program, and even our special favoritism toward it in assigning sugar quotas and the like, did not prevent it from going communist in 1958. Our $769 million of aid to the United Arab Republic did not prevent it from coming under Russian domination. Our $460 million aid to Peru did not prevent it from seizing American private properties there. Neither our $7,715 million aid to India, nor our $3,637 million aid to Pakistan, prevented either country from moving deeper and deeper into socialism and despotic economic controls. Our aid, in fact, subsidized these very programs, or made them possible. And so it goes, country after country.

3. Instead of turning the recipients into grateful friends, there is ever-fresh evidence that our foreign aid program has had precisely the opposite effect. It is pre-eminently the American embassies and the official American libraries that are mobbed and stoned, the American flag that is burned, the Yanks that are told to go home. And the head of almost every government that accepts American aid finds it necessary to denounce and insult the United States at regular intervals in order to prove to his own people that he is not subservient and no puppet.

So foreign aid hurts both the economic and political interest of the country that extends it.

The Unseen Costs of Utopian Programs

But all this might be overlooked, in a broad humanitarian view, if foreign aid accomplished its main ostensible purpose of raising the living levels of the countries that received it. Yet both reason and experience make it clear that in the long run it has precisely the opposite effect.

Of course, a country cannot give away $131 billion without its doing *something* abroad (though we must always keep in mind the reservation—instead of something *else* at home). If the money is spent on a public housing project, on a hydroelectric dam, on a steel mill (no matter how uneconomic or ill-advised), the housing or the dam or the mill is brought into existence. It is visible and undeniable. But to point to that is to point only to the visible gross gain while ignoring the costs and the offsets. In all sorts of ways—economic, political, spiritual—the aid in the long run hurts the recipient country. It becomes dependent on the aid. It loses self-respect and self-reliance. The poor country becomes a pauperized country, a beggar country.

There is a profound contrast between the effects of foreign aid and of voluntary private investment. Foreign aid goes from government to government. It is therefore almost inevitably statist and socialistic. A good part of it goes into providing more goods for immediate consumption, which may do nothing to increase the country's productive capacity. The rest goes into government projects, government five-year plans, government airlines, government hydro-electric plants and dams, or government steel mills, erected principally for prestige reasons, and for looking impressive in colored photographs, and regardless of whether the projects are economically justified or self-supporting. As a result, real economic improvement is retarded.

The Insoluble Dilemma

From the very beginning, foreign aid has faced an insoluble dilemma. I called attention to this in a book published in 1947, *Will Dollars Save the World?*, when the Marshall Plan was proposed but not yet enacted:

"Intergovernmental loans [they have since become mainly gifts, which only intensifies the problem] are on the horns of this dilemma. If on the one hand they are made without conditions, the funds are squandered and dissipated and fail to accomplish their purpose. They may even be used for the precise opposite of the purpose that the lender had in mind. But if the lending government attempts to impose conditions, its attempt causes immediate resentment. It is called 'dollar diplomacy'; or 'American imperialism'; or 'interfering in the internal affairs' of the borrowing nation. The resentment is quickly exploited by the Communists in that nation."

In the 23 years since the foreign-aid program was launched, the administrators have not only failed to find their way out of this dilemma; they have refused even to acknowledge its existence. They have zigzagged from one course to the other, and ended by following the worst course of all: they have insisted that the recipient governments adopt "growth policies"—which mean, in practice, government "planning," controls, inflation, ambitious nationalized projects—in brief, socialism.

If the foreign aid were not offered in the first place, the recipient government would find it advisable to try to attract foreign private investment. To do this it would have to abandon its socialistic and inflationary policies, its exchange controls, its laws against taking money out of the country. It would have to abandon harassment of private business, restrictive labor laws, and discriminatory taxation. It would have to give assurances against nationalization, expropriation, and seizure.

Specifically, if the nationals of a poor country wanted to borrow foreign capital for a private project, and had to pay a going rate of, say, 7 per cent interest for the loan, their project would have to be one that promised to yield at least 7 per cent before the foreign investors would be interested. If the government of the poor country, on the other hand, can get the money from a foreign government without having to pay interest at all, it need not trouble to ask itself whether the proposed project is likely to prove economic and self-liquidating or not. The essential market guide to comparative need and utility is then completely removed. What decides priorities is the grandiose dreams of the government planners, unembarrassed by bothersome calculations of comparative costs and usefulness.

The Conditions for Progress

Where foreign government aid is not freely offered, however, a poor country, to attract private foreign investment, must establish an actual record of respecting private property and maintaining free markets. Such a free-enterprise policy by itself, even it it did not at first attract a single dollar of foreign investment, would give enormous stimulus to the economy of the country that adopted it. It would first of all stop the flight of capital on the part of its own nationals and stimulate *domestic* investment. It is constantly forgotten that both domestic and foreign capital investment are encouraged (or discouraged) by the same means.

It is not true, to repeat, that the poor countries are necessarily caught in a "vicious circle of poverty," from which they cannot escape without massive handouts from abroad. It is not true that "the rich countries are getting richer while the poor countries are getting poorer." It is not true that the "gap" between the living standards of the poor countries and the rich countries is growing ever wider. Certainly that is not true in any *proportionate* sense. From 1945 to 1955, for example, the average rate of growth of Latin American countries in national income was 4.5 per cent per annum, and in output per head 2.4 per cent—both rates appreciably higher than the corresponding figure for the United States.[3]

Intervention Breeds Waste

The foreign aid ideology is merely the relief ideology, the guaranteed-income ideology, applied on an international scale. Its remedy, like the domestic relief remedy, is to "abolish poverty" by seizing from the rich to give to the poor. Both proposals systematically ignore the reason for the poverty they seek to cure. Neither draws any distinction between the poverty caused by misfortune and the poverty brought on by shiftlessness and folly. The advocates of both proposals forget that their chief attention should be directed to restoring the incentives, self-reliance, and *production* of the poor family or the poor country, and that the principal means of doing this is through the free market.

In sum, government-to-government foreign aid promotes statism, centralized planning, socialism, dependence, pauperization, inefficiency, and waste. It prolongs the poverty it is designed to cure. Voluntary private investment in private enterprise, on the other hand, promotes capitalism, production, independence, and self-reliance. It is by attracting foreign private investment that the great industrial nations of the world were once helped. It is so that America itself was helped by British capital, in the nineteenth century, in building its railroads and exploiting its great national resources. It is so that the still "underdeveloped areas" of the world can most effectively be helped today to develop their own great potentialities and to raise the living standards of their masses.

1. See *The United States Balance of Payments* (Washington: International Economic Policy Association, 1966), pp. 21 and 22.

2. Source: Foreign Operations Subcommittee on Appropriations, House of Representatives, July 1, 1970.

3. Cf. "Some Observations on 'Gapology', " by P. T. Bauer and John B. Wood in *Economic Age* (London), November-December 1969. Professor Bauer is one of the few academic economists who have seriously analyzed the fallacies of foreign aid. See also his Yale lecture on foreign aid published by The Institute of Economic Affairs (London), 1966, and his article on "Development Economics" in *Roads to Freedom: Essays in Honour of Friedrich A. von Hayek* (London: Routledge & Kegan Paul, 1969). I may also refer the reader to my own book, *Will Dollars Save the World?* (Appleton, 1947), to my pamphlet, *Illusions of Point Four* (Irvington-on-Hudson, New York: Foundation for Economic Education, 1950), and to my chapter on "The Fallacy of Foreign Aid" in my *Man Vs. the Welfare State* (Arlington House, 1969).

15

Foreign Policy

by Bettina Bien Greaves

And finally, we turn once again to Bettina Bien Greaves for a summary of the main points in favor of a world of voluntary transactions, and the main points against economic nationalism. This essay first appeared in the September, 1979 issue of The Freeman *and like her article on protectionism in Part One was originally aimed at debate students—foreign policy was the subject of the 1979–1980 high school debate resolutions. Since the twin goals of foreign policy are to contain local quarrels and to minimize their recurrence, her analysis shows the importance of free trade in achieving those goals, and pleas for a return to the Jeffersonian policy of no entangling alliances in order to help work for a world that respects private property and establishes borders by legal plebiscite, not by conquest. However, she concludes, "To create such a climate calls for widespread economic understanding. To maintain it would require enternal vigilance."*

Almost everybody wants peace and prosperity. Certainly government officials profess a desire to promote peaceful cooperation among peoples and they devote much time and energy to "international relations." Yet almost daily the press, radio, and TV report international tensions—in southeast Asia, southern Africa, the Middle East, Latin America, or the Orient. As human beings are not perfect, possibilities will always exist for mistakes, misunderstandings, disagreements, and disputes that could grow into widespread conflicts. So the task of those concerned with foreign policy is twofold—(1) to contain local quarrels and (2) to minimize the possibility of such conflicts in the future.

It is natural for people to trade with one another. No doubt men came to understand the advantages of voluntary transactions long before the dawn of written history. Persuading others to part voluntarily with some good or service, by offering them something in exchange, was usually easier than doing battle for it. Certainly it was far less dangerous. Barring force, fraud or human error, both parties to any transaction expect to gain something they value more than what they are giving in exchange. Otherwise they would not trade. This is equally true of trades among friends or strangers, fellow countrymen or foreigners, small enterprises or large—whether located next door to one another or separated by many miles or national borders. Trades may be complex, if intermediate transactions or different national currencies are involved, but the principle remains the same. Both parties expect to gain from a voluntary transaction. So people who trade with one another have both good reason to remain friendly and just cause to resent interferences that hamper or prohibit their trading.

Most consumers care more about the availability, quality, and price of what they buy than they do about who makes it or where it comes from. If a particular gasoline works well in their cars, they don't care whether the oil came from Arabia, Alaska, Venezuela, or Algeria. Consumers will buy Taiwanese shirts, Hong Kong sweaters, Brazilian shoes, German cars, Japanese radios, or any other foreign good, if price and quality suit them. And satisfied customers promote good will.

Economic Nationalism

It is governments, not consumers, that make national boundaries important. It is governments, not consumers, that create national distinctions and promote economic nationalism, often without intending to do so. A tax on U.S. citizens, not required for protecting lives and property or defending the country, increases production costs unnecessarily. Regulations and controls to "protect" consumers, workers, manufacturers, farmers, miners, truckers, the environment, or any other special interest also raise domestic production costs. Benefits to special groups—the unemployed, elderly, handicapped, minority enterprisers, or those awarded lucrative government contracts—must be paid for by others, in taxes or through increases in the quantity of money which in time hurt everyone. All these programs increase costs and make voluntary transactions more difficult and expensive.

As production costs increase, some producers find their sales dropping so they must curtail production and reduce their work force. Many persons then believe it even more important to enact special legislation, erect trade barriers, or grant government subsidies, to support the injured firms and protect them and their workers from foreign competition. But such programs only increase domestic production costs still more. This further hampers the ability of would-be traders to carry out voluntary transactions.

The goal of economic nationalism is to protect domestic producers from foreign competition. Its proponents want to preserve a specific pattern of production. They do not understand the mutuality of trade. They do not realize that both parties gain from a successful voluntary transaction. Nor do they recognize the inevitability of change.

Nothing in this world stands still. People move. The wishes of consumers change. Their knowledge is continually shifting. Changes also take place in stocks of available resources and the most economical places in which to produce particular items. Producers, investors, and workers should be free to move about and adjust to these many changes as best they can.

Any attempt to maintain, for political reasons, some rigid pattern of production is bound to fail. Insofar as production is guided by political, rather than economic, motives, it becomes more expensive and wasteful. When government seeks to reduce dependence on imports and increase national self-sufficiency, consumers must get along with fewer goods and services of lower quality; and their standards of living will decline.

Foreign Policy Repercussions

Restricting imports by government fiat reduces exports also. How can foreigners continue to buy as much from us, if our government restricts their opportunities to earn dollars by selling goods in this country? The mutual gains that come from trading turn traders into friends. But when trading is hindered, ill will has a chance to develop. Frustrated would-be traders look for someone or something to blame. Officials of foreign governments become antagonistic to the U.S. government, for they realize their producers' sales to this country are hampered by our government's interference. However, few U.S. citizens blame their government for imposing trade restrictions. Many even consider the federal government a benefactor. For when imports and exports decline the federal government often tries to make up for lost trading opportunities by offering those who are hurt direct or indirect assistance—subsidies, relief, new protective regulations, and so on. But such government programs can never compensate would-be traders fully for opportunities forgone, reduced production, and the loss of individual self-respect.

The advocates of free trade pointed out more than a century ago that "if goods do not cross borders, soldiers will." As fewer exchanges take place across national borders, individuals have fewer opportunities to know and respect one another. Antagonism, animosity, and enmity among nationals may arise. We have seen this happen in recent years—in India and Pakistan, Southeast Asia, the Middle East, southern Africa, and elsewhere. Obstacles to the path of trade made transactions across national boundaries more and more difficult, expensive, and infrequent. The common bond which could have turned their international traders into friends was weakened. Those who could have helped each other through voluntary transactions had no cause to come together. They remained strangers and, in time, were even led to consider one another enemies.

Government intervention, which begins by distinguishing between domestic and foreign goods and producers, leads in time to a policy of economic nationalism which actively discriminates in favor of domestic products to the disadvantage of imported goods. This hurts not only foreign producers, whose goods are excluded from the domestic market. It also harms domestic consumers and producers. Production costs rise so that fewer goods can be produced and sold. With fewer goods and services available for everyone, living standards decline.

Localizing Conflicts

The sure way to turn local disputes into widespread conflicts is for outsiders to interfere. The first step in that direction often springs from a sincere sympathy on the part of the strong for the weak, the "rich" for the "poor," the "haves" for the "have nots." Officials of one nation offer to help defend a weaker country against the threats of stronger neighboring states. But by taking sides in this way, neutrality is abandoned. No matter how well-intentioned, such government-to-government economic aid and mutual defense agreements show favoritism which can lead in time to military actions and wars. Through U.S. commitments such as NATO, SEATO, and SALT, as well as various treaties, pacts, and executive agreements—relating to the Middle East, China, Russia, Panama, Japan, various African nations, and more—we could well become embroiled in local violence or border disputes, at almost any instant, almost anywhere in the world.

U.S. involvement in the Middle East undoubtedly began with a sincere sympathy for Jewish refugees who wanted to establish a homeland in Israel. Our involvement in Vietnam has been traced by some to a desire to help relieve France, when she was economically and financially strained by military operations in her colonial Indochinese territories, so as to persuade her to join NATO. "We do not plan our wars; we blunder into them" as history professor Henry Steele Commager has pointed out.

George Washington's advice in his Farewell Address (September 17, 1796) is still sound: " . . . nothing is more essential than that permanent inveterate antipathies against particular nations, and passionate attachments for others should be excluded, and that in place of them just and amicable feelings toward all should be cultivated . . . The great rule of conduct for us in regard to foreign nations is, in extending our commercial relations, to have with them as little *political* connection as possible." And similarly, Thomas Jefferson urged "peace, commerce, and honest friendship with all nations, entangling alliances with none" (First Inaugural Address, March 4, 1801).

U.S. involvement in this century in two World Wars as well as Korea and Vietnam is due to the fact that U.S. foreign policy has been guided by precisely the opposite ideas from those Washington and Jefferson advocated. To contain local violence, a nation should avoid taking the first step toward abandoning neutrality and playing favorites. Thus, we should refuse to add to the many international commitments our country is now duty bound to honor. Then we should move toward the foreign policy recommended by our third President— "peace, commerce, and honest friendship with all nations, entangling alliances with none."

Minimizing Future Conflicts Through Free Trade

To minimize conflicts in the future we should aim to create a world in which people are free to buy what they want, live and work where they choose, and invest and produce where conditions seem most propitious. There should be unlimited freedom for individuals to trade within and across national borders, widespread international division of labor, and worldwide economic interdependence. Would-be traders should encounter no restrictions or barriers to trade, enacted out of a misguided belief in economic nationalism and the supposed advantages of economic self-sufficiency. Friendships among individuals living in different parts of the world would then be reinforced daily through the benefits they reap from buying and selling with one another. Thus a sound basis for peaceful international relations would be encouraged.

Individuals should have the right of national self-determination and even to shift national political boundaries, if they so voted in a plebiscite. For practical and economic reasons, a single administrative unit would be sovereign within the political borders so established. But this administrative unit would have to be responsive to the wishes of the people or face being ousted in the next election. It would have to do its best to protect equally the private property of every inhabitant and to respect the rights of all individuals within its borders, irrespective of race, religion, or language. In such a world, members of racial, religious, or linguistic minorities need have no fear of political oppression for being different. Any nation which adopted these policies at home and in its relations with other nations would help to reduce international tensions and so contribute to minimizing future conflicts. But once it began to play favorites again—to grant privileges to some to the disadvantage of others, to introduce restrictive controls and regulations—it would be re-embarking on the path that leads to friction and conflicts among individuals, groups, and nations.

World Peace

To maintain peace throughout the world, the grounds for conflict should be reduced as much as possible. The first step in this direction must be to respect and protect private property throughout the world. The ideal would also include complete freedom of trade and freedom of movement. Political boundaries would no longer be determined under threat of military conquest or aggressive economic nationalism, but rather by legal plebiscite, i.e., by vote of the individuals concerned. In such a world, the national sovereignty under which one lived and worked would be relatively immaterial.

Daily news reports certainly indicate that we are a long, long way from approaching this ideal. Programs intended to promote world peace often lead in the opposite direction. The various intergovernmental institutions—the United Nations and the several regional political and economic communities—do little or nothing to reject economic nationalism. The debates and proposals of their representatives reveal little understanding of the mutual advantages private traders gain from voluntary transactions. They do not even appear to consider the possibility of leaving trade to private individuals and enterprises to arrange as they see fit. Rather they continue to delegate important powers to various governmental authorities to regulate and control quantities and qualities of imports and/or exports, sometimes even to set minimum or maximum prices at which certain commodities may be traded. In their desire to protect various fields of production within their newly erected borders, they foster economic nationalism over geographical areas larger than a single nation. Thus, although the spokesmen for these multinational organizations sometimes talk of "freer trade," their actions lead to less free trade.

The foreign policy that would minimize future conflicts would promote an economic climate in which voluntary trades among private individuals would flourish because private property was protected worldwide. To create such a climate calls for widespread economic understanding. To maintain it would require eternal vigilance.

Bastiat, Frederic. *Economic Sophisms.* Translated from the French (1851) and edited by Arthur Goddard. Irvington-on-Hudson, New York 10533: Foundation for Economic Education, Inc., 1964.

Bauer, P. T. *Dissent on Development: Studies and Debates in Development Economics.* Cambridge, Massachusetts: Harvard University Press, 1972.

Curtiss, W. M. *The Tariff Idea.* Irvington-on-Hudson, New York: Foundation for Economic Education, Inc., 1953.

Fleming, Harold M. *States, Contracts and Progress: Dynamics of International Wealth.* Dobbs Ferry, New York 10522: Oceana Publications, Inc., 1960.

Krauss, Melvyn B. *The New Protectionism: The Welfare State and International Trade.* New York, N.Y. 10003: New York University Press, 1978.

Mises, Ludwig von. *The Free and Prosperous Commonwealth: An Exposition of the Ideas of Classical Liberalism.* Translated from the German (1927) by Ralph Raico. Edited by Arthur Goddard. Princeton, New Jersey: D. Van Nostrand Co., Inc., 1962. Reprinted 1985 as *Liberalism: In the Classical Tradition.* Irvington-on-Hudson, New York: Foundation for Economic Education, Inc. and San Francisco, California: Cobden Press.

Epilogue
Peace or Politics

by Frank Chodorov

P eace is the business of Society. Society is a cooperative effort, springing spontaneously from man's urge to improve on his circumstances. It is voluntary, completely free of force. It comes because man has learned that the task of life is easier of accomplishment through the exchange of goods, services and ideas. The greater the volume and the fluidity of such exchanges the richer and fuller the life of every member of Society. That is the law of association; it is also the law of peace.

It is in the market place that man's peaceful ways are expressed. Here the individual voluntarily gives up possession of what he has in abundance to gain possession of what he lacks. It is in the market place that Society flourishes, because it is in the market place that the individual flourishes. Not only does he find here the satisfactions for which he craves, but he also learns of the desires of his fellow man so that he might the better serve him. More than that, he learns of and swaps ideas, hopes and dreams, and comes away with values of greater worth to him than even those congealed in material things. . . .

The law of association—the supreme law of Society—is self-operating; it needs no enforcement agency. Its motor force is in the nature of man. His insatiable appetite for material, cultural and spiritual desires drives him to join up. The compulsion is so strong that he makes an automobile out of an oxcart, a telephone system out of a drum, so as to overcome the handicaps of time and space; contact is of the essence in the market place technique. Society grows because the seed of it is in the human being; it is made of man, but not by men.

The only condition necessary for the growth of Society into One Worldism is the absence of force in the market place; which is another way of saying that politics is a hindrance to, and not an aid of, peace. Any intervention in the sphere of voluntary exchanges stunts the growth of Society and tends to its disorganization. It is significant that in war, which is the ultimate of politics, every strategic move is aimed at the disorganization of the enemy's means of production and exchange—the disruption of his market place. Likewise, when the State intervenes in the business of Society, which is production and exchange, a condition of war exists, even though open conflict is prevented by

137

the superior physical force the State is able to employ. Politics in the market place is like a bull in the china shop.

The essential characteristic of the State is force; it originates in force and exists by it. The rationale of the State is that conflict is inherent in the nature of man and he must be coerced into behaving, for his own good. That is a debatable doctrine, but even if we accept it the fact remains that the coercion must be exercised by men who are, by definition, as "bad" as those upon whom the coercion is exercised. The State is men. . . .

Getting down to the facts of experience, political power has never been used for the "general good," as advertised, but has always been used to further the interests of those in power or those who can support them in this purpose. To do so it must intervene in the market place. The advantages that political power confers upon its priesthood and their cohorts consists of what it skims from the abundance created by Society. Since it cannot make a single good, it lives and thrives by what it takes. What it takes deprives producers of the fruits of their labors, impoverishes them, and this causes a feeling of hurt. Intervention in the market place can do nothing else, then, than to create friction. Friction is incipient war.

About the Foundation for Economic Education

The Foundation for Economic Education, founded in 1946 by Leonard E. Read, exists to serve individuals concerned about freedom. Recognizing that the real reasons for freedom are grasped only through an understanding of the free market, private property, limited government way of life, The Foundation is a first-source institution providing literature and activities presenting this point of view.

• *The Freeman,* a monthly study journal of ideas on liberty, has been published by the Foundation since 1956. Its articles and essays offer timeless ideas on the positive case for human liberty and criticisms of the failures of collectivism. *The Freeman* is available to anyone upon request. (The extra costs of mailing to any foreign address require a minimum charge of $10.00 per year.)

• Our annual catalogue, *A Literature of Freedom*, carries a wide range of books and audio cassette tapes on a variety of topics related to the freedom philosophy. More than 120 volumes are currently available from the Foundation.

• FEE's seminar program is designed to bring individuals together to better understand and communicate free market ideas. In addition to three week-long seminars at FEE each summer, several one- and two-day sessions are offered at FEE and at different locations in the United States. The seminar faculty, composed of FEE staff members and guest lecturers, cover economic, philosophical, and historical topics. Discussion sessions provide valuable opportunities to question and explore ideas.

• High school and college students—We actively encourage the study of free market ideas in high schools and colleges in a number of different ways:

On-campus lectures by FEE staff members. Groups vary in size from small classes to school-wide assemblies. Lectures are always followed by a question and answer session.

Seminars in Irvington. Each year FEE hosts three weekend seminars for selected undergraduates from around the nation. These seminars present a solid introduction to free market economics and the philosophy of limited government and individual responsibility.

Debate materials. FEE assists high school debaters by preparing a collection of free market materials covering the current national debate topic. More than 1,000 of these booklets are distributed annually.

Freedom essay contest. An annual conpetition for students with cash awards for winners. Prize-winning essays are published in *The Freeman.*

For a student subscription to *The Freeman,* or to inquire about any of our other student programs, please write to FEE.

The costs of *The Freeman* and other FEE projects are met through tax-deductible donations. The financial support of more than 12,000 individuals permits the Foundation to distribute its publications widely and to advance the prospects for freedom in America. Join us in this important work!

For further information, write:

The Foundation for Economic Education, Inc.
Irvington-on-Hudson, New York 10533